With Consent:

parenting for all to win

by Jan Fortune-Wood

"... I'm going to show ... a world without rules or controls, without borders or boundaries, a world where anything is possible. Where we go from there is a choice I leave to you."
(*The Matrix*, closing scene, spoken by the character, Neo.)

Educational Heretics Press

Published 2002 by Educational Heretics Press
113 Arundel Drive, Bramcote Hills, Nottingham NG9 3FQ

British Cataloguing in Publication Data

Fortune-Wood, Jan
       With Consent:
       Parenting for all to win
       1.Parenting 2.Education 3.Autonomy in children
       4.Education – Philosophy 5.Education – Aims and
       Objectives
       I.Title
       370.1

ISBN   1-900219-24-7

Design and production: Educational Heretics Press

Cover design by John Haxby, Edinburgh EH6 6QH

Printed by Mastaprint Plus Ltd. (Tel. 0115 939 1772)

Contents

Acknowledgements

Thanks are due to many people who have helped this book to take shape, whether directly or through inspiration. Thank you to Roland and Janet Meighan, whose support, encouragement and friendship has remained constant. Thank you to all the friends who have read drafts, given me feedback and offered valuable criticism; especially Peter Tuffnell, Sue Cvach and Stella Howden. Thank you to the TCS community, those people who write on the Internet list and in the journal, and who are a constant source of rich ideas and growth of knowledge and most especially to Sarah Lawrence, founder of TCS. Thank you to the home-education community, especially to all those who attend the annual gathering known as HES FES, the world's largest home education camp, organised by Andy Blewett; to everyone who attends my workshops and asks questions.

Above all, an enormous thanks to my family, my husband Mike and our four children. *Taking Children Seriously* has been a theory that has enormously enriched our lives, but only because the whole family have given so much creativity, thought and criticism to how we can constantly improve our living and learning together.

Jan Fortune-Wood
June 2002

Introduction

In *Doing It Their Way* (EHP April 2000) I wanted to propose that real education is about the intrinsic motivation of autonomous learners; in other words children learn best when they are supported in following their own interests. In *Without Boundaries*, I set out to expand on this theme, arguing that both in theory and in practice, coercion is not only destructive of personal autonomy, but also inimical to learning and the growth of knowledge. Two years later and thanks to all those who have bought *Without Boundaries* and offered valuable feedback, I am exploring this theme again in a second edition, *With Consent*.

Put simply, children can and should have their own way. Madness, impossible, dangerous, a crackpot utopian idea? I want to suggest to you that children should get what they want and that, far from producing spoiled brats who will exhaust you with their demands, rob you of any life of your own and then want more, helping your children to get what they want in life will also mean that you the parent will fulfill your preferences too. You can all live together well when you are living by consent. What parent has not longed to improve his or her relationship with children? What parent has not thought to herself, 'Surely, there must be a better way than this', but felt defeated and trapped by old ways of relating? This book is about that better way. It is not magic; relationships are demanding, complex things, but imagine that all of the energy you have ever used on fighting your children, cajoling your children, begging your children, coercing your children, even hurting your children, could go instead into finding solutions with them; solutions that they want, solutions that you want; solutions in which everyone is a winner. Unbelievable? No, merely rational and creative.

The radical parenting ideas that you are about to consider are born out of the *Taking Children Seriously* philosophy of parenting and education. This worldwide theory, founded by Sarah Lawrence, proposes that in place of coercion we can reach common preferences with children, that is, win-win situations that respect and nurture the autonomy of children. The book falls into two sections, with a concluding chapter drawing the themes together. The first part sets out a theory of non-coercion as it relates to parenting and learning. The first chapters examine the terminology *of Taking Children Seriously* and the role of parents. Chapter three is new, looking in more depth at entrenched parental theories and particularly at the theory of memes, before chapter four explores autonomy as the basis for true growth of knowledge.

The second section looks at how the theory relates to autonomous learning and parenting practice. It takes an in-depth look at the issues that arise in any transition to an autonomous process and is focussed on the idea that with non-coercive techniques, all participants can be 'winners', using illustrative scenarios to demonstrate the point. In the central chapter of the book, the vital theme of 'learning to win' is explored through a number of issues in family life and learning; the emphasis to the positive effects of taking children seriously; not simply living non-coercively, but actively seeking solutions and new knowledge. The final chapter sums up this quest and looks at the how this learning philosophy can be applied across age ranges, individual personality differences, amongst families where members have been labeled with learning difficulties or syndromes or live with disabilities, and in situations where formal, structured education, including schooling, is viewed as an option by young people.

The *Taking Children Seriously* (TCS) philosophy, which is the inspiration of this book, is a wide-ranging theory that cannot be fully encompassed within the confines of such a short book. I hope to offer an introduction to a way of thinking that could revolutionise how we parent and how we think about learning. In a world where parenting manuals proliferate, *With Consent* offers a radical and practical alternative - not only a new paradigm for parenting, but one which deals with how, in a fast-changing world, parenting and learning must be integrated.

Part 1:
A theory of living with consent, not coercion

In this book I want to argue not only that eradicating coercion is fundamental to real learning, but, more importantly, that we can live together as families so that everyone can win. I want to argue that children should get what they want, that adults should also get what they want and that both are mutually compatible. The book assumes a philosophical context developed by the founders and thinkers of *Taking Children Seriously*, a rational philosophy that replaces coercion with common preferences - that is, solutions that everyone really prefers. In a world of sacrifice, martyrdom and enforced distress, the idea is as extraordinary as it is practical: we can get what we want, parents and children; we can all win and learn from doing so.

Conventional parenting theories, whether disciplinarian or liberal, are everywhere. Most of us want parenting advice that is eminently practical, but trying to find another way of parenting is like entering a whole new world. We do well to take a breath and re-orientate ourselves. The way we think about our children and our relationship to them, and the way we speak to and about our children, make all the difference to the way we act. Conventional parenting advice comes with a whole raft of often-unquestioned thinking, assumptions and ways of talking. Consent-based parenting is new. It encourages us to ask the previously unasked questions, to take apart thoughts that have seemed to be obvious or common sense so that we can overcome the obstacles to living in families where everyone wins.

You do not need to be mastermind or take a course in theoretical philosophy to be a parent; anyone can have a child and it is not always the most well-educated who make the best relationships with their children. On the other hand, if you want to discover how to parent so that everyone wins, you need to do a bit of thinking and you need to be prepared to go on thinking, challenging yourself at every stage, and staying constantly open to learning and growth in the parenting adventure.

In this first part of the book I want to introduce you to that other world, the world of consent. I will do this in two ways. Firstly, I will explain what *Taking Children Seriously* means, so seriously that you do not act against their wills, but value and respect their autonomy to the utmost. A child getting what it wants is not about neglect. It is not about never making suggestions or offering criticism or about children who never change their minds. In fact, changing our minds is crucial to the creativity needed to find good solutions, and that goes for parents, too. This is easier said than done. At some point, we all find ourselves hard up against deeply ingrained patterns of thinking that stop us from finding solutions and leave us feeling trapped and frustrated. Why? We all have our own areas of coercion damage. We all have certain ideas that run so deep that we find them hard even to notice, let alone criticize and change.

Secondly, in chapter three, I will look more closely at the obstacles in our way, the ideas that prevent us from living by consent. These things are very personal. Most conventional parents agree that there are certain things that require coercion, yet no one agrees about what those things are. Perhaps you have no hang-ups about bed-times, room tidiness, watching TV and eating sweets, but feel that the world will end if teeth are not brushed twice a day every day, so that you will coerce your child if you cannot convince her?

These deeply rooted ideas, which are often less than rational in the way they are thought about and expressed, rely on what the scientist Richard Dawkins has called 'memes'. Memes are ideas that reproduce themselves in much the same way as genes reproduce themselves in the biological realm. In chapter three I want to explore with you the idea of memes: what they mean for our parenting, how they might affect us and how we criticize those that place obstacles in the path to consent.

Consent-based parenting is another world of thought. We need to adjust our thinking to its differences. We need to know what obstacles lie in our path so that we can be ready to revolutionize our relationships to our children and live together so that everyone wins.

Chapter one

Taking children seriously

How is it possible to live family life without compromise? How can we always have win-win situations? How can responsible parents let go of the notion that issues of safety require parental law enforcement? First, we have to think that it is possible.

In the film *Pleasantville,* two modern day teenagers are transported into a television drama of a romanticised and constructed world of 1950s small town America, a golden age in glorious black and white. Everyone knows their place. There is no change, no books, and no new ideas – instead, everything is pleasant. The outsiders - one at first unwittingly, the other with intent - bring with them new thoughts. Gradually things change; most notably, colour begins to appear. The town elders, shaken at the loss of control and anxious about where all these new ideas might lead, try to ban colour, but the genie is out of the bottle. At a town meeting, one of the teenagers defends the changes:

> *"... I know you want it to stay pleasant around here, but there are so many things that are so much better, like silly or sexy or dangerous or brief and everyone of those things is in you all of the time if you just have the guts to look for it ..."*
> (*Pleasantville,* New Line Cinema Production. A Time Warner Company)

Consent-based parenting is similarly as full of possibility - silly and dangerous included - if we are to acknowledge that learning involves trial and error, conjecture and refutation, mistakes and growth. It is full of possibility for growth and new knowledge. To move our parenting from monochrome to technicolor parenting, we will need to know how to begin, especially in areas where it has previously seemed to be self-evident to us that coercion is necessary. We will need to know how to think and speak in this colourful, messy world. Taking children seriously is not a dogma or doctrine to live by, but a philosophy that gives us tools to help find creative, rational solutions that enable everyone to win.

Coercion damages thinking

Perhaps you think that coercion is harmless? Perhaps you think that certain acts of coercion are obviously wrong and harmful - you would never beat your child, but a tap on the hand when a toddler is about to touch a fire is surely the lesser evil? Most of us think that there are degrees of coercion. We draw lines that we would not cross; stiff talking to, being grounded or losing pocket money might seem to us mildly painful, but useful ways of motivating good and responsible behaviour and of showing ourselves to be caring and responsible parents. Most of us think that coercion is inevitable. We might wish life could be sweetness and light, but still tell ourselves that sometimes you have to strap your toddler in the buggy to make that important appointment on time or refuse to buy another computer game for your teenager so that you can pay the gas bill.

Such acts of coercion, we tell ourselves, are the normal stuff of life that all of us have to be able to accept and get over quickly. Well, they are certainly commonplace, but I want you to think again - not so that you can wallow in guilt, which is a worthless and demotivating emotion, but so that you can live differently now.

Meet Alex. Alex is a lively four-year-old who has been brought up in a caring, busy family. He has an older sister, Jenny, who is seven, and a baby brother, Jack. His Dad works long hours, sometimes away from home overnight, and his Mum, Emma, is beginning to feel over-tired. Baby Jack likes to do some of his feeding at night, but tends to have a long sleep in the evening from around eight o'clock. Jenny, tired out by school, happily settles down by eight in the evening and Emma thinks this would be an ideal time for her to get some extra sleep on those evenings when her partner, Steve, is away from home.

The problem is Alex. Alex has never seemed to need a great deal of sleep. He has only recently begun to sleep through the night, but he simply will not settle down as early as eight in the evening and, to make matters worse, he also wants to be up early in the morning. Emma is at the end of her tether. She is worn out and often feels bad tempered and resentful with Alex during the daytime. Emma reads the books and consults her friends and knows that it is Alex's intransigence that is causing her all these problems and everything would be much better for everyone, Alex included, if she could go to bed early two or three times a week. Everyone tells her that she has to get tough with Alex, for his sake and her own, and teach him that he has to go to bed at a 'reasonable' hour and stay there until a 'reasonable' hour.

We can all sympathize with Emma. Being at home with young children, doing the lion's share of childcare and feeling sleep-deprived into the bargain are not made any easier by being commonplace. Of course, Emma needs more sleep and needs to get her preferences met. The mistake that conventional parenting theories, friends and Emma are making is to decide in advance that there is one solution and that this solution is so important that it is worth coercing Alex - even believing that the coercion is as much for Alex's benefit as anyone else's. Later on, I'll return to the subject of finding solutions in tight corners like this one, but for now I want to concentrate not on the many possible solutions to this situation, but on Alex and the damage that may be being done to him.

We have to admit that we do not actually know what the damage is. The problem with coercion is that it affects every unique individual in uniquely individual ways. Some children are seemingly impervious to what might look like horrific and substantial coercion. Other children can be put into states of turmoil and emotional pain from what seem to be very minor and everyday acts of coercion. One child triumphantly proclaims *"That didn't hurt!"* as she is smacked for the tenth time that day, while another whimpers at the slightest cross look from his mother. It is for this reason that we cannot establish an acceptable quota of coercion that can be safely used on children.

It is rather like a pregnant woman drinking alcohol. In theory, there is no safe amount. That does not mean that one glass of champagne at your best friend's wedding is definitely going to harm your baby. It is simply that we cannot actually know whether some miniscule or slightly larger damage might occur for that particular fetus at that particular stage of development or whether there will be no effect at all.

Coercion is something that happens in the mind of another human being and it is not always clearly apparent; when we talk about coercion damage, we are not talking about something measurable and uniform. We cannot predict that one smack will result in 2% thinking damage, or that six months of being forced to go to bed at a particular time will result in 4% thinking damage. Humans are simply not that predictable. What we can say is that every act of coercion risks some damage that will be unique to each individual and that repeated acts of coercion in one area will tend to produce damaged thinking of varying kinds in that area. Alex may be a very resilient little boy, but it is just as likely that he will experience considerable distress at this new regime and that, even though he is eventually defeated, he also suffers from forgetting how to live by his own body clock, growing up with poor theories about how much sleep is needed regardless of personality and individual requirements. Later in life, Alex may well develop sleep problems without ever knowing why.

Life is full of things to blame. If our children behave badly or grow up as unhappy individuals, we have a ready list of culprits to reach for: sugar, E numbers, food allergies, pollution, TV, computers, syndromes like ADHD or Asperger's, peer pressure, schools, the decline of the church, the breakdown of community, changing standards of discipline or a thousand and one other bogeys. It is obvious that parents, for the most part, care passionately about their children and do everything in their power to do their best for them. Amongst so many competing pressures, it seems cruel and unhelpful to blame parents for their thirty-year-old son's sleep problems or alcohol use. This book is not a charter for blame, guilt or spurious psychobabble to make parents responsible for every little action of every child aged 0-90. It is about how we can live best in this moment, realizing that we will have made mistakes in the past and that we will make mistakes in the future, but finding optimistic and creative ways to do no harm or consistently do less harm and more good. In the vast majority of cases, even the most coercive parents are not bad people who want to harm their own children, but loving, passionately involved parents who want to do their best for their children. This book is not a call to condemnation, but simply a plea to look at coercion differently, to see it not as your ally in childraising, but as potentially deeply damaging and surmountable.

To begin to think of coercion differently we need a different language. When we talk about 'taking children seriously', what, exactly, do we mean? We're talking about key ideas such as:
- *non-coercion*
- *rationality*
- *fallibility*
- *creativity*
- *criticism*
- *theories*

- *common preferences*

We are talking about turning the world of parenting upside down, so it is worth taking the time to think about these basic ingredients of living by consent. These are the tools of revolution.

Coercion

What do we mean by coercion? The shorthand *Taking Children Seriously* (TCS) definition is

> *"anything that causes a person to enact one theory whilst another theory is still current in their mind".*
>
> (**www.tcs.ac** © Sarah Lawrence)

A child washing up whilst she really wants to climb a tree, a child who is made to put on a track suit to go shopping when he wants to go in his pyjamas, or a child doing homework when she really wants to be watching her favourite TV show, would be obvious examples. Coercion, though, is not always obvious. Perhaps the child working through a science workbook has been told by her parents to clean the rabbit hutch. The child wants to watch *The Simpsons,* but the parent is adamant that the hutch needs cleaning now, so the child responds that she was actually planning to get on with her science homework. The parent approves and agrees that this is a more worthwhile activity, at least for the time being. In the parent's hierarchy of activities, cleaning rabbit hutches should not interrupt science homework any more than TV watching should interrupt pet care. The child is left enacting one theory (doing homework) whilst another theory (watching TV) is active in her mind. She is in a state of coercion, even though she suggested doing the homework. If this persists, she is likely to develop thinking difficulties about science and pet care and cleaning and TV. How can she think clearly and rationally about these things when her mind is so full of coercion and tangled subterfuge?

Coercion can be direct or it can be subtle and manipulative. Children want their parent's love and approval. Whenever love and approval are conditional, whether the condition is getting a high score in a spelling test, eating cabbage, or only watching parentally condoned television shows, there is coercion. Anything that is done against the child's will, that causes the child to do or think x while he still wants to do or think y, is coercion. Coercing runs the risk of causing damage and puts us in the bad position of compromising the autonomy of another human being and is best avoided.

That is not to say that we will always succeed, but we need to realize that we can no longer justify coercion as a last, necessary resort. If we do, then we will sabotage the whole attempt to move into consent-based living. Children cannot trust that they have moved into a non-coercive environment or that it is in their interests to join in with the process of finding solutions if they know that the bottom line is that the parent reserves the right to coerce. In order to be willing to be open-minded and available to the possibility of change, children need to be confident that they do not have to come up with a solution that fits into the parental notion of necessary action. If we coerce by mistake, children will understand our humanity and fallibility. If we coerce because we reserve the right when all else fails, we are stuck with conventional parenting.

So what does non-coercion mean?

- Children not being forced to enact one theory (e.g. washing dishes, getting in the car, putting on clothes etc) whilst another theory is active in their minds (e.g. watching TV, playing with Lego, staying in pyjamas etc).

- Children not being forced to resort to subterfuge in order to avoid certain coercion (eg offering to take the dog for a walk rather than do household chores when the child really wants to be climbing a tree).

- Parents avoiding behaviours that cause one theory to be enacted while another is active in the child's mind. (We are not just talking about those overt things like smacking or forcibly moving a child or confining a child to a room. Many of us parents develop a skillful repertoire of disapproving glances, sighs and postures that our children understand all too well.)

- Parents not reserving coercion as a last line of defence. (Consent-based parenting is only going to work if your children can trust that your advice is your best theory, not just a backdoor method of control.)

Rationality

When we talk about coercion damage, we are not talking about the bruises an abused child receives in a violent home, but about something that takes place in the mind of the child. Coercion has the potential to affect how people think about things. The turmoil of having one theory active in his mind whilst being made to do something else affects how Tom thinks about those things; things like eating, playing, learning. That is where rationality comes in.

Rational thinking is about having the space to engage genuinely in a search for the truth. To achieve this, there must be the possibility of refutation as well as conjecture, and openness to criticism both from oneself and from the theories of others. If parents cut short their children's searches and experiments by asserting that they have superior authority or experience, then the rational process is interrupted. Parents who have information or opinions on a subject should be able to contribute to the rational argument; if their arguments fail to convince, perhaps they should be willing to give way to new and better theories.

There is often a tendency to believe that reasoning is something that develops with maturity and experience, and is dependent on our ability to construct an articulate argument. This kind of thinking allows that we can 'reason' with older children according to their age and developing intellectual capacity, but not with babies, toddlers and young children who are pre-verbal or have more limited articulacy and logic. Being rational and being able to reason is not the same thing as having a certain level of articulacy, intellectual development or leverage through verbal logic. A baby constantly creates new knowledge and, as such, is a rational being. We can find common preferences with any rational being. We may not always use words. We may sometimes use very simple words with visual and practical demonstration, but we will definitely be aware of a baby or toddler's preference. We can also clearly see that toddlers and babies are able to move to new preferences or (in their own way) suggest new solutions to adults.

It is sometimes assumed that if finding common preferences is a rational process, then it must be acceptable to employ this process to coerce a child who is deemed to be acting irrationally. This is not the case! It may be true that a child's thinking has been damaged by coercion and so in certain areas a child may be acting irrationally. This damage does not justify further immoral intrusion into the child's autonomy. Adding more potential damage through more coercion is not a solution. Even more importantly, it is very hard, if not impossible, to look into another mind. We cannot say with any degree of certainty whether behaviours are the result of irrationality caused by coercion damage or if they might actually be very good theories which deserve our consideration, but, because of *our own* irrationality, we find them hard to follow. Getting into such psychological guessing games is both futile and destructive. We do far better to simply meet each theory with criticism and creativity, without using pejorative and dismissive labels against our children.

Rationality, then, is a vital element in living by consent. It entails:

- Each individual's search for truth by conjecture and refutation
- An openness to criticism from oneself and others
- The ability to change theories
- The ability to make new knowledge at all ages and stages of life
- The ability to find solutions to problems (whether it is a toddler figuring out how to undo a bottle or teenager composing music)
- Not trying to guess what is in the minds of others by labeling certain theories or behaviour 'irrational' and so dismissing them (yes, you *might* be right, but you cannot know for certain and more coercion will not help you!)

Fallibility

One thing that greatly assists non-coercive parents is recognition of their own fallibility. If we take seriously the possibility that we might be wrong then we are much less likely to attempt to compel our view onto another, even when we strongly believe that it is correct. Fallibility is central to parenting with rationality and consent. Our theories may well be right, but we can never know that as an absolute certainty. We should always be open to the possibility that the other person, even if she is a distressed two-year old, has a better theory. Fallibility is another major factor in achieving consent - remember: 'you may be wrong, even when you know you're right.'

Creativity

Another crucial element in finding consent-based solutions is creativity. Creativity is simply the ability to problem-solve in ways that create new knowledge, resulting in new theories which are useful and relevant to everyone concerned. Creativity is the ability to move from one state of mind to a preferred state of mind. It does not require that we are all creative geniuses before we take up parenting. As the TCS website entry on this subject puts it:

> "... Building a satisfying life is itself a creative endeavour. Developing good moral theories is a creative endeavour. ... Creativity plays a part in all improvement in each and every area of life. Coercion impairs creativity. This is not limited to the narrow sphere which is often called 'creativity'..."
>
> (TCS website www.tcs.ac © 1997-99, Sarah Lawrence)

Consent-based parents have to get creative and their children's creativity is also important. It is simply about:

- Finding solutions
- Changing minds
- Making new knowledge

Criticism

Along the way, rationality and creativity are aided by criticism. That is not an invitation to disparage your child's arguments or to engage in dismissive denigration. A feature of taking a child seriously is to engage with her ideas, point out problems and make genuine contributions. When there is no compulsion on the child to accept the criticism, it can soon be seen as a gift that is available for evaluation.

Criticism requires that we share:

- The best theories, opinions, morals, information and suggestions that we have available
- That we offer our criticism without compulsion
- That we remain open to the possibility that our criticism may be wrong
- That we do not keep repeating the same criticism ad nauseum, long after our children have asked us to desist

Theories

The TCS philosophy uses the word 'theory' very broadly, to indicate any state of mind or being or disposition that is active within a given person. Theories can be conscious or unconscious, explicit, inexplicit, inborn, inherited or learnt; but none are immutable. Our theories can change.

Let us consider Ellen. After a lifetime of coercion, most which would be considered petty by the casual observer and nearly all of which has been in the name of her own good and best interests, Ellen grows up and becomes a parent. She is convinced that children need to eat a very careful diet to keep them healthy. According to Ellen's best theory, this is a diet that is sugar free, additive free and vegan. Her child has other ideas, and months, if not years, of conflict and misery follow while Ellen imposes her 'essential' food theories on her son. It may be that Ellen has some good and rational ideas about eating, but she has become incapable of thinking openly and rationally about food. No amount of reason or criticism is going to convince Ellen that her son's brain and health do not require this particular and strict diet. Ellen's friends offer other good ideas. Ellen can see that they have certain logic to them. She can see that her friends' children do not appear to be suffering from the poor nutrition, lethargy or bizarre behaviours that she feels a wider diet would lead to, but she still cannot bring herself to let go of her enormous fear that without a controlled diet her child will suffer. Ellen's theories are entrenched. Parenting is a practical activity - it involves actions, but those actions rely on our thinking. Our theories matter.

Ellen's practice as a parent is completely controlled by food theories that she cannot even begin to evaluate herself. All of us have areas where our thinking is far from clear. All of us hold some theories that are so deeply entrenched that they present obstacles in our way, often without our ever realizing that this is the case. This is a theme to which we will return in detail in chapter two, but for now we simply need to realize that our thinking matters when we are parents. Theories count.

- Theories are anything from morals to opinions to tendencies
- Theories can be very deeply entrenched, sometimes so deeply that we do not even articulate them; they are unquestioned assumptions.
- Theories can change, especially when we engage them with rationality and creativity and recognizing our fallibility

Common preferences

A key feature of any family following a consent-based philosophy is the practice of finding common preferences. This is any solution to any problem that all the participants agree is preferable to either their original solutions or to any other solutions that have been considered. A common preference implies a win-win situation in which everyone is pleased with the outcome. It is not a compromise in which one solution wins whilst others give way, reluctantly or sadly or with the poor option that they will get their turn to win another time. Common preferences rely on genuine consent. They also rely on the ability of the participants to change their original preference during the process of problem solving. This does not mean that original preferences are never followed. Sometimes the original preference of one person may turn out to be the common preference of all, but unless there is a basic willingness to change and explore new ideas, no common preference can be reached.

Finding mutually desired solutions demands both rationality and creativity and the basic belief that solutions do exist to problems, even if we do not always find them.

Within families, we are not used to win-win scenarios with everyone on the same side. We are used to assuming that often, if not always, someone must lose, that compromise is about as good as it gets, and that conflict is inevitable. This is not a utopian book and I am not advocating an elite parenting theory for perfect people or for parents chronically addicted to sacrificing themselves to their monstrously demanding children, but I can tell you that common preferences work. They work in large and small families, poor and rich families, families from every cultural and ethnic background, families with and without adherence to particular faiths, families with one parent or two parents or gay parents or living in communities. Common preferences work wherever there is a fundamental trust that children are rational and creative, wherever there is the essential realism to admit that we are all fallible and therefore need to proceed on every issue with an open mind, wherever we are willing to devote our time, energy, and resources to consent, instead of to conflict and damage. Then, everyone can win.

Common preferences also require another basic assumption. In order to enter into the process of finding common preferences with our children, we have to believe that a child getting 'what they want' is not the opposite of moral living and caring about others. Children expressing their preferences are simply doing the right thing for themselves, which may very well be the thing that also has great benefits for others as well. Why should we think that, given autonomy, our children would choose evil? It is a fear that is false and which needs questioning at every turn.

Common preferences, then, are the final essential ingredient of consent-based parenting - parenting so that everyone wins. When we talk about common preferences, we mean:

- Solutions that everyone *really* prefers (**not** compromises)
- Solutions that have the consent of all parties
- Solutions that are found when everyone is open to engaging rationally, using creativity and contributing their criticisms and theories

- Solutions that are found when those involved are willing to change their minds (though that does not meant that first suggestions never become common preferences)
- Solutions that take seriously that everyone getting what they want is a good thing.

Morality

Taking children seriously is a moral issue. Coercion is not always immoral, but for our purposes we are thinking about the relationship of parents and children. Parents have a special responsibility towards the children they bring into the world and that responsibility includes the obligation not to harm their children. Coercion of children by parents risks harm. We cannot always guess when the harm will occur. We cannot quantify the harm, but we can conjecture that it does do very real harm to children's ability to learn and be their full rational and creative selves.

TCS also assumes that parents will share their best moral theories with their children. How do we find these best moral theories? By a process of conjecture and refutation with a constant acknowledgement of our fallibility. TCS is not a relativist philosophy, i.e. it does not support the idea that competing moral theories are just a matter of choice and lifestyle. The assumption is that Truth exists, that we can use our reason to deduce the right thing to do, but of course knowing that Truth exists and believing that we have come to some final formulation of it are entirely different things. Fallible humans are alike in boundless ignorance and we can hold ideas only tentatively. In short:

- There is objective moral Truth
- We can deduce morality by conjecture and refutation, but should be tentative in assuming that we have found the truth
- We should do our fallible best to share our best theories of morality with our children
- Coercion, of itself, is not always immoral
- It is immoral for parents to harm their children and coercion risks harm

A new world

Amongst liberal parenting theories, there are a wide variety which would claim to take children seriously. What this often means is listening to children and taking account of children's views, but without necessarily giving them equal weight and with no commitment not to coerce the children in the final decision. Only TCS philosophy goes further than this. It proposes a whole new paradigm for interaction between parents and children, to reach solutions in which children's autonomy and right not to be coerced is fully respected. It is a paradigm that tends to evoke strong responses and a barrage of questions. Is it not it likely to lead to neglect? What if the child wants to engage in all sorts of dangerous or immoral behaviours? Surely the parents end up as slaves to every childish whim with no time or energy to do what they want in their own lives? These and many other questions will be explored in the following chapters. What is important to assert from the outset is that TCS is an eminently practical philosophy precisely because every family tailors it to their own lifestyle and preferences. It is also, I believe, the only theory of parenting and education which fosters truly autonomous education since it places the emphasis squarely on the child's intrinsic motivation and does not fall prey to the lure of products and outcomes.

For those of us who have already taken the step of putting our children's autonomy centre stage in their education, particularly within the home-education community, the realisation that life will never be the same again is generally not slow in dawning on us. Valuing educational autonomy soon leads to massive shifts in lifestyle. I am convinced that it is only TCS that adequately answers the lifestyle and parenting questions that arise from a commitment to autonomous education. TCS is not, however, exclusively the preserve of home-educating parents. There are many for whom the need to find alternative parenting practices which eradicate the stress of continual conflict and uneasy compromise from their lives come before any consideration of educational theory. The chapters that follow will, I hope, be of equal value, however the approach is made. One thing is certain; life with TCS will challenge every assumption you have ever made.

Chapter two

The parental role

So where do parents fit in? As I have already stressed, this book is not a recipe for neglect or permission for parents to 'let the kids get on with it.' As parents, though, we do have to re-appraise our roles.

A non-symmetrical relationship

Parents have power over the children they brought into the world, and they have obligations to those children that the children do not have in return. This power is boosted by the natural desire of children to want their parents' approval and liking. Parents decide to have children. The children have no say in this and do not enter into any form of contract to obey the parent merely by the act of being born. Parents, on the other hand, do have a moral obligation towards their children. They are obliged to care for and help their children.

This does not mean that taking children seriously is merely a matter of 'giving way' to every suggestion a child makes; rather, it is a matter of finding common preferences with the child. It is only in the event of the failure of the process of finding common preferences that a parent should 'give way'. In reality there are always solutions out there (the theoretical possibility of solutions) but we do not always find them. We are, however, more likely to find solutions the more we practice using our creativity in this way. Remember though, this is not a symmetrical relationship in which children owe you in the same way that you owe them. You are the parent; get used to it.

The trusted advisor

In a consent-based household, the parent is a source of morality, advice, information and criticism. Living consensually does not mean that we should never make suggestions about information, activities, foods or anything else. It does not mean keeping our advice to ourselves, unless the child has heard it a hundred times and asks us to refrain from repeating it.

Sharing our theories is an important - in fact, vital - parental role, but we can only share our own best theories. These may be very good or they may be completely fallacious. Sharing them will be a good thing as long as we accept our own fallibility and do not expect sharing to lead to compliance. We can even share theories about things which are highly personal - like hair colour, bodily odour, room tidiness - provided that we are prepared to accept that in the final analysis some things are simply a matter of bodily autonomy. A useful rule of thumb is that if we would not expect an adult friend to comply, then we have no right to expect compliance from a child. Of course, Ben might welcome the tips about personal hygiene before his first date, in which case there is a common preference. If we are willing to acknowledge our own fallibility and if we are able to restrain ourselves from insisting, even when we are convinced that we are right, then our children are most likely to learn to look upon us as trusted advisors. They will realize that we do not know everything and that we sometimes speak unadulterated rubbish. Despite this, they will still be more than willing to ask for our opinion, to hear us out, to engage with our ideas, to listen to and weigh up our criticisms, knowing that they can do so without fear of coercion or loss of autonomy.

When the role of trusted advisor is working well and our children really trust that it will not lead to coercion, it is likely that parents will be given far more access to their children's lives than conventional parents would have. After all, lying or secretly engaging in dangerous behaviour without ever seeking advice are not necessary to a child whose parents are not going to say 'no' on principal, holding on to parental authority or threatening punishment.

Mutual solutions

Our theories, information, moral views and criticisms are gifts, but it is ultimately for the recipient to make best use of the gift. A scary thought? Well, parenting is scary, but living by consent, far from increasing the fear, reduces it with good reason. When we insist that our theories should be followed and when we threaten punishment or consequences, (however 'liberally' conceived), if our theories are not accepted, we are risking damage to our child's ability to think rationally and openly about the subject in hand. How can a child listen to rational arguments about teenage sex or eating chocolate or jumping from a ten-foot wall onto concrete if she really knows that ultimately the decision will be forced from her, or she will have to resort to deception? If we offer information and theories that are good, then a child who is used to being taken seriously will see the logic of our argument on its own merits. If our argument is unconvincing, then perhaps more information is needed, or the child has a better theory, or we are simply talking about a matter of taste and choice.

Coercion and protection

Of course we want to protect our children and of course we want to be responsible parents, but consider: coercion might not be a responsible course of action. Will coercion ultimately keep children safe? What right have parents to thwart a child's will in order to achieve the supposedly good end of protecting them? So how do we keep them safe? Whether the protection is physical or verbal, it still requires that a common preference be found. Parents generally have a greater pool of life experiences to draw on. This can lead us to believe that we 'know best' or have a duty to coerce 'for the child's own good'. *This is not the case*. Parents undoubtedly have more experience than children. Sometimes this will mean that we have good theories. It will also mean that we have accepted hundreds of bad and conventional ideas about children and parenting and have had our own thinking and rationality damaged by the coercion done to us as children. Experience is something that parents have to offer, but it is not always rational. Offering experience with acknowledgement of our fallibility is a far cry from deciding that we know best. Furthermore, children, although they lack experience, may be fortunate in having their rationality less clouded by years of coercion and faulty assumptions.

We can offer our experience, without assuming it is infallible or universal. We can offer our best theories, without presuming that we are correct, even if we deeply believe that on this occasion we are. We can give information and help our children to find other sources of information. Ultimately, having children who understand the decisions they are making as fully as possible and know how to find out more information is eminently safer than having children who obey while their parents are there to impose their wills, but act in the dark as soon as they are on their own. From sharp tools to fires to staying out alone, there are assumptions about externally imposed safety rules shared by conventional parenting, but I want to argue that these actually compromise safety by stopping children from coming to their own rational decisions about personal safety.

Imagine two nine-year-old friends, Thomas and Luke. They are enjoying exploring a piece of woodland near their homes when one day they wander further and come across a derelict building. The building is boarded up, but not securely, and they can wriggle inside. As they enter they pass the notice 'do not enter, risk of falling masonry'. The building is full of wonderful hiding places and a great set for imaginary adventures. Luke suggests they spend the day exploring the building and keep it their secret. Thomas already has a hundred ideas for games they could play in this new den, but says they should ask an adult to check that it is safe. He says that he knows that old buildings like this do move or have rotted floorboards that give way under people. Luke replies that Thomas is 'chicken'. He insists that they will be fine and that adults are always telling children lies to stop them having fun. He also points out that if he asks his parents about playing here they will just say no without even looking at the building and get mad with him for going in the first place. Thomas objects that his parents do not tell him lies and like him to have fun. He says his Dad knows quite a bit about buildings and will be able to tell them how to play safely or find other ways for them to have a cool den if this building is really dangerous. Luke says angrily that adults do not help children, they just tell them what to do.

It is the child who has been brought up with rules who is much more in danger. Luke's information about the world is much less reliable that Thomas'. Luke's parents do not see fit to give him all the information; he just needs to know what he can and cannot do. Luke also knows that not everything his parents tell him is true, he knows that they exaggerate or even fabricate to keep him in line, but he cannot always tell the bogus from the vital information. Luke's parents have replaced information with rules, but Luke's desire to engage in illicit behaviour is also increased by the rule-bound mentality. He sees his parents as the enemy and here is a chance to outwit them. This attitude makes no sense to Thomas, who, living in a TCS home, sees his parents as trusted advisors who will only give information that they really believe themselves and will help Thomas to find other opinions too. Thomas knows that whatever his parents think of this particular building, they will help him find a way of having a den and getting to play the games he and Luke want. Thomas knows that his parents would help him make his own mind up as though he were a serious person, not a silly idiot. Luke, on the other hand, sees an opportunity to indulge in an activity that would be forbidden and that is so important to him that he cannot think about the dangers or his friend's weird notion that adults help children. If Luke is wrong about the building, he could be in real danger. If Luke is right on this occasion, it is simply by chance, not rational thinking, but this will only serve to entrench his idea that adults are not to be consulted, which could mean danger for Luke, perhaps when he is fifteen and experimenting with drug use alone.

Having a child who will seek our advice before playing in a potentially dangerous place or conducting experiments with electricity or making their way out of an upper storey window is a great asset to safety, a subject to which we will return in chapter 7. Life and risks are intrinsically bound together. Sometimes we choose risks quite rationally in order to learn something or enjoy some particular experience. This said, there are many dangers that are avoidable. The safest course is to parent our children so that they will trust our advice, critically assess our best theories and make their own rational decisions.

Neither laissez-faire nor self-sacrifice

Let us be quite clear: abandoning children to their own devices, without the constant input of information, moral beliefs and the gift of criticism, is a failure of parental duty. Laissez-faire parenting is simply a liberal form of coercion in that children are denied access to parental care and help. TCS parents are very engaged parents. They do not simply 'leave their offspring to it', they ensure that their children have what they need to make well-informed decisions about their lives.

So, if it is not neglect, and our children are getting what they want out of life, then surely they can only be doing so at our expense? The assumption that parents and children are always in some way opposed and competing is false. Consent-based parenting is not a call to parental self-sacrifice. What we are aiming at is consensual living, and that means everyone, even you, the parent, being happy with the solution. In fact, people generally find that when they begin eradicating coercion from their relationships with their children, they are also less willing to live with coercion in other areas of their lives. I will return to the theme of self-sacrifice more fully in chapter 5, but for now it should be noted that self-sacrifice is never the aim or seen as a good outcome. What is fair to say is that parents who take their role and their children seriously believe that in the event that no common preference is found, it is better to self-sacrifice than to coerce. It is something to be reflected on and improved upon. It is not a good solution, but one that should and will be used less and less as we become practiced at creative problem solving. In the longer term, children will be very happy to have a creative model of finding common preferences, which they know will serve them in continuing to get what they want as they move into adulthood. The future will look as flexible and full of possibility as the present.

Consider Sophie, aged three and her Mum, Lucy. Lucy grew up with a very self-sacrificing and highly coercive mother. Her mother did everything for her all the way through childhood, and her mother complained continually about how she did everything and was just used by her family and unappreciated. Lucy did not learn to do any cooking at home; her mother said she would only make a mess and burn things, though no one ever let Lucy find out if this were true. She left home having never cooked an egg, hardly having ever boiled a kettle, not having a clue about washing her clothes and struggling to cope at college on her own.

Lucy is now a mum herself. She does everything for Sophie - after all, she is so little. Lucy wants to be a good Mum and unlike her own mother, Lucy does not resent her daughter. Two things have happened in Lucy's life: she has heard about *Taking Children Seriously* and consent-based parenting, and she has been offered some part-time work doing research at home. Both appeal to Lucy, but Sophie is used to being served in every way. Sophie is a bright, happy little girl with lots of energy and interests. Lucy feels she should be able to sit at her computer and get on with some work for parts of the day, but Sophie calls on her continually.
"I need a drink, Mummy."
"Switch my video on, Mummy."
"I'm hungry, Mummy."
"Take me to the toilet, Mummy."
What is more, Lucy has noticed that Sophie's wants are very immediate, in that she wants what she wants and she wants it now. Despite all her vows never to end up like her own mother, Lucy can feel herself getting resentful, sometimes even snapping sharply when Sophie does not want to 'wait a minute' and then resenting all the extra time taken because Sophie gets upset.

Lucy talks to a TCS friend, who makes some helpful suggestions. She could buy some plastic jugs that Sophie can hold, fill them with her favourite drinks and water and keep them on a low refrigerator shelf that Sophie can reach. She could teach Sophie how to operate the video and TV controls and how to go to the toilet alone. She could spend some time in the morning with Sophie preparing snacks that Sophie likes and putting them in accessible places. She could change the times when she works to evenings or weekends

when Sophie's Dad can do something for fun with Sophie while
Lucy has quiet. She could offer to look after Sophie's best friend
two afternoons a week in exchange for the same favour from the
best friend's mum on another two afternoons. Lucy does not have to
become Sophie's slave. It is quite likely that her daughter would
enjoy being able to do at least some of these things for herself, but
Lucy does have to think creatively, not simply give up.

The voluntary parent

If you think that finding common preferences sounds like a lot of
hard work, try asking yourself which form of parenting offers you
an easy life. Parenthood carries responsibilities, but there is no
need to see those responsibilities as terrible burdens. We must stop
treating our relationships with our children as exacting demands and
start enjoying them. We are sadly mistaken if we become parents
thinking that there is an easy option. Relationships take work.
Important relationships can take lots of work, but what would you
rather work at – thwarting your children and constantly struggling
to maintain control, knowing that it is going to take a lot of negative
conflict along the way; or helping your children to get what they
want and getting your own preferences met, realizing that it is going
to take a lot of creativity? Trying to live by consent entails
parenting in a counter-culture way which will demand that you are
constantly creating new knowledge. That is hard work and
sometimes difficult to implement, but it is also an enormously
satisfying and optimistic way to live.

Parenthood carries responsibilities, but that is not the same as
sacrifice. If I pay for a holiday, I do not think of the money I have
used as being sacrificed. I weigh up whether this is what I want to
do with my money, but, having made the decision, I do not resent
what I am giving up to get the longed-for holiday. The giving up is
voluntary, a simple way of getting something that I prefer and can
enjoy more than the money in my purse. Children are not
commodities, of course, and the analogy is limited; but, for parents,
giving up certain aspects of a life without responsibility is not a
sacrifice, but a change to a new and preferred state.

We should enter into parenting with an intention to promote our
children's autonomy, delighted when we can help them get what
they want from life, and thrilled that we can facilitate their growth,
learning and happiness by their own lights. This is not a burden or
a sacrifice, but a parental preference. When we can start thinking
and feeling like this, parenting ceases to be the chore that many

conventional parenting theories would have us believe that it is. It is a sad reflection on our notions of parenting. (and perhaps on our concept of relationships in general), that we conflate something which takes a lot of creativity, risk, learning, and openness with being something sacrificial, burdensome, and an occasion for resentment. The two do not have to go hand in hand. A swimmer who sets her heart on swimming a distance in a particular time has to devote a lot of energy, commitment and creativity to achieving her goal. She does so willingly. She is happy to alter radically her diet and to devote her time to realizing her desire. Her goal is challenging and difficult, but it still remains voluntary - her most important preference and a joy to execute. When we are able to see our relationships with our children like this, and not as onerous and tiresome, then we will not grudge the creativity and time that we put into finding common preferences. Rather, we will be exercising our own preference to help someone we chose to bring into the world. Finding mutually preferred solutions is not galling, but delightful.

Parenting with consent

Parents are not left without a role. On the contrary, they have a wide-ranging and important role in their children's lives, but the ground has shifted from conventional terms.

- Parenthood comes with responsibility. You owe your children, they do not owe you.
- The consent-based parent is a trusted advisor – share your opinions, give your criticism.
- Remember the decision is theirs and you could be wrong.
- Information and trust keep children safer than rules.
- Leaving your children to get on with it for themselves is just neglect; consent involves engagement.
- If you feel like a doormat, start to think you are a martyr or cannot remember what it is like to have a preference about something, then you are self-sacrificing and no one is going to win.
- Self-sacrifice does not only make you resentful, it stops your children from thinking that consensual solutions can be found and gives them a poor picture of parenthood.
- If consent sounds like hard work, it is, but it is a more pleasant work than fighting you child for sixteen years.
- We can learn to think that helping our children is a pleasure, not a chore.

Chapter three

A matter of ideas

What stands in our way of living lives of consent? Most of us think that the obstacles are practical ones: we do not have enough time for all this creativity, we do not have enough money to satisfy our children's preferences, we are not good at problem solving. We tell ourselves that our children are too young to be rational or that they have sugar allergies or soft teeth that mandate that we cannot just let go of the controls on their diet. The truth is that all of these practical problems or so-called absolutes are soluble. It is not the practical difficulties that block the path, but our own ideas and theories.

Changing ideas

Practical problems do not stop you from helping your child to get what he wants; ideas do. It is your theories that get in the way of living by consent with your children, not schedules or the number of hours in the day or the need to go to work or the amount of money you have available or any other practical consideration. The problem is not the practical difficulty, but the way we think - our creativity, our ideas.

Imagine Paula. She is at the airport with her five-year-old daughter, Zoë, half an hour away from boarding her flight from London, where her parents live, to Texas, where she lives. Suddenly, Zoë announces that she has left her favorite teddy bear at Grandma's house and she wants to go back to fetch it. Most of us in this situation think that the problem is one of time: we cannot retrieve the bear and board the plane and it is obvious to any adult which of those things has to happen. If Paula is a conventional parent then she is probably willing to offer comfort to Zoë, as long as Zoë does not make too much noise in a public place, but Paula will also believe, like most parents, that Zoë has to learn that some things just cannot be changed. Some things just have to be done whether we like them or not. Some things are simply not negotiable.

The real problem, though, is not the conjunction of practical factors - an airplane departure at 8.30a.m, a mere round trip of 40 minutes and a distressed child do not add up to an impossible situation in which someone has to lose. The real problem is Paula's inability or unwillingness to think that there is a solution. The solution might very well involve a later flight. It is not actually an immutable law of nature that Paula and Zoë must get on this plane. Although, as parents, we often present our decisions as though there really were no choice, as though our doctor's appointment or need to do some grocery shopping was written into the universe, the truth is that there are choices – as many as our creativity allows us to envisage.

The solution might include Paula's initial preference that she and Zoë board their flight on time. Perhaps there is a story that they could invent together to make the bear's absence an extra stay with Grandma so that she does not have to say good-bye to them all at once, or a story to make the time it takes for the bear to be posted to Zoë an adventure. Perhaps a new toy from the airport shop would make all the difference. Perhaps a call to someone at Grandma's house or to a courier service could get the bear to the airport in time. Perhaps Zoë simply needs more information – information about how much extra new plane tickets would cost, using up money she might like for other things, and information about how Daddy will be waiting at the airport and will be sad not to see them for another day. Such information is not to be used to manipulate Zoë with guilt and sentimentality, but it is real information that she can choose to take into consideration, knowing that the final decision has not already been made.

If Paula is a TCS mother, she will tell Zoë that she really prefers that they make this plane. She will tell Zoë why that is her preference – things that she hopes to be able to do by being home at a particular time, people who are meeting them at the other end, extra expense and what that might mean to their family, effects on their tiredness and ability to enjoy an already long journey. She will make suggestions about alternatives – stories about the bear, a new toy, a trip to the ice-cream shop at the airport, the possibility of someone bringing the bear to the airport for them and how they will deal with it if the bear does not arrive on time. Zoë, knowing that her mother wants to find a common preference, a way in which both of them can win, will be able to listen and consider without feeling brow-beaten, knowing that she does not have to sit on the airport floor and cry her heart out to get listened to.

Let us imagine that Paula is this TCS mother and she and Zoë find a solution. They decide to ring Grandma and ask her to post the bear, but they also ask Grandma to take some pictures of the bear at Grandma's house, the bear being packaged, the bear being handed in at the Post Office. Zoë and Paula take pictures together of their journey and decide to keep a scrapbook of pictures of things they do when they get home until the bear arrives so that they can make their own picture narrative of the days of the bear's adventure. In the meantime, an ice-cream, a large cuddly Dalmatian toy from the airport gift shop and the thought of Daddy waiting to meet them mean that Zoë decides that getting on the plane now is actually what she wants to do.

A couple of years later, Paula is at home with Zoë and her new baby, Jacob, when Jacob suddenly develops a high temperature and begins to convulse. The hospital is close to their home and Paula knows that she can drive there quicker than an ambulance would take to reach them and get back again. Zoë has just got a new Playstation game and Paula knows that Zoë really does not want to leave the house today, but neither is Zoë comfortable alone at home. Paula has noticed that both sets of friendly neighbors, who might otherwise sit with Zoë, have gone out today. Paula tells Zoë that this is an emergency, she does not have time to talk this through right now, and Jacob needs to get the hospital. This is a very rare moment for Zoë. She knows that her mother does not lie to her, that Paula does not decide outcomes before discussions, so, despite not otherwise wanting to go to the hospital, Zoë has no qualms about accepting the genuineness of her mother's fears for Jacob and leaves her game without a backward glance.

Ideas, not practical problems, are the real blocks to living by consent. Solutions are out there, but we do not always find them because we do not always have ways of thinking about them. We all have inner voices that say 'you cannot always win' or 'but teeth have to be brushed no matter what children want' or 'if Jimmie watches too much TV he'll become aggressive'. We all have areas in which our theories are very poor indeed, often because of the coercion we have experienced ourselves or because the ideas which we learnt and imitated are, in fact, false. These ideas can become so strongly held that they are 'entrenched', so that, sometimes even reason seems unable to affect them.

These deeply rooted ideas often rely on memes, self-replicating ideas which transmit from brain to brain. We are not slaves to these memes. We can work to change them, but first we have to identify the enemy. What is a meme?

Meeting memes

The scientist Richard Dawkins was the first to propose the theory of memes - ideas that, like genes, are self-replicating:

> *"The new soup is the soup of human culture. We need a name for the new replicator, a noun which conveys the unit of cultural transmission...*
>
> *"Examples of memes are tunes, ideas, catch-phrases, clothes, fashions, ways of making pots or of building arches. ... memes propagate themselves in the meme pool by leaping from brain to brain via process, which, in the broad sense, can be called imitation."*
>
> (From *The Selfish Gene* by Richard Dawkins. Chapter 11)

For our purposes, Sarah Lawrence describes how the notion of memes relates to parenting:

> "Memes *are ideas which are replicators. In other words, any idea (or theory, or attitude, or skill etc.) which is passed from one person to another through behaviour (i.e. not by genes) is a meme. You might think of it as the psychological analogue of a gene.*
>
> *"Whether something is a meme or not depends on how it is transmitted, not on its content per se. So, for example, shyness or fear of making a fool of oneself are not, in general, memes because they suggest coercion-induced irrationality rather than ideas which might be replicators. The coercive parenting ideas that led to the shyness or fear of making a fool of oneself might well be replicators, though. And if that fear plays a role in causing the parents to hold those ideas and coerce their children in a way that makes them acquire the same fear, then the fear itself is part of the meme.*
>
> *"Whenever parents behave in ways that cause their children to grow up behaving in ways that cause their children to grow up to cause the very same behaviour in their children ... a meme is operating."* (www.tcs.ac)

In short, memes are self-replicating ideas passed from brain to brain via behaviour and the imitation of behaviour. Memes exhibit the features of evolution. They are inherited in that they are copied. They vary in that the copying is not exact, but is subject to subtle and larger mutations through imperfect copying. There is a process of selection in which the memes that survive will tend to be those that are highly memorable, useful or provoke an emotional response.

The human arena of parenting is full of memes. Most of us have sworn never to be the kind of parents that our own parents were to us, and yet most of us soon acknowledge that there are deeply rooted parenting ideas that come from having been practiced on as children. Whether against our better judgement or not, we will often discover that many of our deepest held parenting theories bear more than a passing resemblance to those of our families and to the dominant theories of our particular culture. Even when we rebel, we may often find that we are doing little more than buying into the same meme (or memeplex) from another angle.

Imagine Denise, for example. Denise grew up with a mother who had strong ideas about 'other people'. Denise's mother, Margaret, was firmly of the opinion that life was a competition that she and her family were fated to loose. Margaret was convinced that other people outside her family were intent on putting her down. Her own coercive childhood and lack of education had led Margaret to develop these ideas and, as a protective mother, she wanted to do all that she could to stop Denise from getting hurt in the world.

Margaret felt that she would be doing her daughter no favours to expose her to too much interaction. If Denise showed an interest in a hobby or pursuit, Margaret would seem initially interested and supportive, but she would soon begin suggesting that Denise might not really enjoy herself at ballet or horse riding or drama group. She might find it hard and look silly, she might have an accident and hurt herself, she might not make friends there and then she would feel like an outsider. When times for taking part in the activity came close, Margaret would soothingly tell Denise that she need not go if she really did not want to. She would sympathetically say that she understood that Denise did not really like to be around too many people and should not force herself to go. On later occasions, Margaret would also refer to previous incidents to back her theory that Denise had a history of not being able to cope with groups. *"Remember how you thought you'd go horse riding, but when it came to it you couldn't face all those strangers. I know you'd like to try things, but you always find groups so difficult. It's fine to stay home with me. Maybe you shouldn't get involved with anything else."*

In time, Denise became more withdrawn. She learned the meme that competition leads to failure and humiliation not because she failed herself, but because she was too convinced by the ideas transmitted to her to even risk trying. Now Denise is a young mother and very protective of her four-year-old daughter, Helen. When Helen attempts to climb on the frame at the park, Denise hovers around, full of dread, constantly saying *"be careful"*, *"don't climb that high"*, *"mind you don't hurt yourself"*. She notices that in interactions with other children, Helen is always the child who has toys taken away from her or who hangs back on the edge of the group. Denise wants to help Helen have more enjoyment, but she is unaware of herself saying things like, *"It's only a toy, Helen, play with something else." "Never mind, darling, some people are like that, you just stay away from them." "You don't have to go to Sophie's birthday party. I know you don't really like parties."* Although Denise wants to help her daughter, she is acting out a meme that has passed down generations and, at four, Helen is learning not to expect too much from life and not to try to change things.

Patrick, on the other hand, is a father who believes that he has been able to stop a harmful meme in its tracks. Both of Patrick's parents were alcoholics, but Patrick feels he has taken control of his life. Unlike his drunken parents, he never drinks and is relaxed around his wife and friends who drink moderately with meals. Patrick's thirteen-year-old son, Hugh, also likes to have wine at family meals and so far Patrick has conceded that Hugh can drink in this way. Patrick, however, is far from relaxed about this. He talks to his wife, Gemma, about having a no-alcohol policy in their home, fearing that Hugh might have inherited a tendency to alcoholism from his grandparents.

Patrick believes he has beaten the meme of alcoholism, but in fact he is still playing it out. He sees the world through the lens of this meme, categorising people as good, tolerable and bad on the basis of their relationship to alcohol. Patrick believes that Hugh is incapable of using alcohol for benefit and pleasure because he will be inevitable taken under its control. He is very close to imposing this meme on Hugh and is probably already doing so in subtle ways, like treating Hugh's glass of wine with a family meal as a huge concession, and by being obviously tense when he gives Hugh information about alcohol, and by behaving in subtle but powerful ways that suggest that Hugh will turn out to be the passive prey of alcohol, rather than an autonomous and creative individual.

Patrick has rejected his parents' outward behaviour. He is not an alcoholic. He is still engaged, however, in transmitting the meme that some humans, (in this case members of his family), are unable to handle alcohol without becoming addicted. He is still behaving in ways that could cause Hugh to take on the idea that people are defined by alcohol and incapable of regulating its use for themselves; an idea that Hugh may go on to transmit to his children in turn, even if, like Patrick, he avoids alcoholism.

Are memes so in control of our ideas that we can do little more than imitate the memes handed on to us by our parents or by our culture or by some appealing and apparently counter-cultural trend? Or can we come to recognize and criticize memes? I believe that we can rebel. We can use rational criticism to weigh the memes by which we operate in parenting, and in other areas of our lives. Even parents can change! To say that we are our memes, our ideas, just as we can say that we are our genes, is not to negate the existence of the self or to collapse into a predetermined world without freewill. Memes make up the ideas that we need for creativity and they are essential to the ideas we have about ourselves. It is mistaken and simplistic to assert that the power and influence of memes is such that there is no free will. Parents are certainly acting under a range of memes that may largely have been transmitted to them without their knowledge or consent, but we are still able to interact with ideas rationally and creatively.

Let us return to Patrick. Fortunately, Patrick is married to Sandra, who has heard about TCS and is convinced that parenting can be something she had never before imagined, a matter of consent. Sandra disagrees when Patrick suggests banning alcohol from their home. She suggests to Patrick that by making such an issue out of alcohol, even when he thinks he is being terribly liberal and tolerant, what he is actually doing is dramatising the subject and attributing all sorts of special powers to alcohol that Hugh may never have thought about otherwise.

Patrick can see that alcohol is a subject he finds it difficult to think rationally about. When he thinks back on some of the apparently casual comments he has made to Hugh about drinking, he agrees that if Hugh were to continue the same ideas and pass them on to his children, then the meme that alcohol has irresistible power would still be alive and well in his family three generations on from his own alcoholic parents. Patrick agrees that it would be a very good thing to stop this meme and that the fact that he has not himself become an alcoholic like his parents is not sufficient. He decides not to interfere with anything to do with alcohol. From now on, all conversations and information about alcohol will be between Hugh and Sandra. Sandra and Patrick acknowledge that even this tactic may have the undesired effect of elevating alcohol as something out of the ordinary, but agree that this is the first step to improving the chances of ridding their family of the meme.

- Memes, though not intentional, have the evolutionary urge to survive and propagate.
- Memes can have a powerful effect without our awareness or consent.
- Memes are of differing kinds: some harm us; some are neutral and others are beneficial.
- Although we may often be unconscious of the memes we are promoting and propagating, we can become conscious of our memes.
- The selection process of memes and the decision-making powers of ourselves as hosts are not alternatives, but co-exist.
- This means that we are not just victims of replicating ideas competing within us. We have human creativity and rationality; the ability both to change memes and to change the memes that we operate from.

Beware of memeplexes

Memes are powerful. Blind processes of selection drive them and memes can survive without our knowledge or even when we are indifferent to or opposed to the ideas they carry. This is particularly true of 'memplexes', ideas that group together to support one another. Examples of memeplexes are religions, ideologies and lifestyles. The memes form groups of ideas that self-replicate together, giving support and complexity to particular dominant theories. Memeplexes will often contain rational and useful memes that aid our attempts to parent by consent, but they will also contain false and harmful memes that inhibit our thinking about children or lead to their being taken less seriously or treated stereotypically and wrongly. In parenting, as in other areas of life, we need to have a critical eye on the memeplexes as well as the individual memes.

One common memeplex that occurs repeatedly in parenting is that of common sense. A huge amount of coercion and poor thinking is justified in the name of common sense. It is common sense that children have to learn to do as they are told, that children have to go to school, that children have to wrap up warm in cold weather, that a child who does not learn to read by the age of ten is going to fail in life, and so on. Many of the memes that band together as 'common sense' and that aid one another's survival by this alliance are questionable or false, but it is equally false merely to write off whole memeplexes. The common sense idea that we should not jump out of twenty storey buildings without a safety net is good advice that is not made less good by being lumped together with false common sense ideas. In other words, when we are dealing with memeplexes, it pays to be selective. We may want to reject the religion of our childhood or the political dogmatism of our parents, but it is worth sifting through the generations of memes that have survived for some reason to see which contain nuggets of truth.

Let us take Susan. Susan has adopted a 'natural living' memeplex that has greatly influenced her parenting. In this memeplex, it is essential that babies are breastfed, carried everywhere (rather than pushed in prams or pushchairs), sleep with their parents for as long as they desire, use only cloth diapers, wear natural cotton clothing, play with toys made from natural materials such as wood, not be exposed to TV and new technologies, and eat a whole foods diet which particularly excludes refined sugars and processed foods. All seems well for Susan with her first baby, Pip, who seems to respond positively to this lifestyle.

Later, Susan has another child, George, and also hears about TCS. Susan begins to think about the idea that she should be treating her children as unique individuals rather than according to a particular stereotype of what may or may not be 'natural'. This is a difficult concept for Susan, who has set up her life to do what she had thought was the very best for her children. She also finds that this second baby presents his own challenges to her former ideas. He is very unsettled in her bed, cries often and only appears to settle on the odd occasions when he is not held. George also suffers from constant nappy rashes, despite Susan's great care over cleaning and only using environmentally friendly washing powders. In desperation, she tries disposable diapers and the rash soon clears up (just the opposite of Pip who would get a rash on the rare occasions that Susan used disposables). Susan begins to dramatically question the whole memeplex of 'natural living and parenting'. The more questions she asks, the more disenchanted she becomes with her former philosophy. She feels very skeptical of even being able to define what true natural living might be at any particular moment in time and in any given culture.

It would be very tempting for Susan simply to throw out the whole memeplex, to believe that anything that she once thought natural is just a bogus control technique, but she would be wrong. There are some important insights within the natural living memeplex. When Susan has her third baby, Amanda, carefully sifting through individual ideas in the light of the unique person that Amanda is, will greatly help Susan to take her daughter seriously and to benefit from useful memes. It so happens that Amanda, like Pip, has the kind of skin that prefers cloth diapers and it certainly seems that Amanda, like most babies, loves to breastfeed. Meanwhile, Amanda's older brothers are now benefiting from a house in which there is always plenty of fruit on hand, which they love, but where they can also access the sugary snacks they like too. Pip and George still enjoy their wooden toys - in fact, Pip is beginning to show his own interest in woodworking - but that does not stop the boys from also enjoying Playstation games.

Susan no longer believes that living by the memeplex of 'naturalness' is the best way to parent her children, but she can also see that the memeplex that she once thought held all the answers does in fact have some very valuable insights along with some very coercive ideas.

- Memes group together to enhance their mutual survival.
- Groups of memes, known as memeplexes, are transmitted in the same way as individual memes.
- Memes survive for a reason, even if they are false and harmful.
- Memeplexes aid the survival of the memes that group together.
- Within memeplexes there are both true and false ideas.
- When a particular memeplex is rejected there will still be good and useful ideas that are worth retaining.

Changing entrenched ideas

How do we criticise memes and decide which are good or bad, true or false? We do so by using our rationality and creativity, through a process of conjecture and refutation. If some memes are bad - even dangerous and harmful - then that might lead us to believe that some memes should be suppressed, especially in our children. Linda, for example, is an active feminist who wants her daughters to appreciate their own self-worth and to be able to feel confident and equal to any situation. To do this, however, she thinks that it is a good idea to limit their access to books and TV shows that stereotype girls and women or which portray violence against women. Linda knows that bad ideas can do harm, so she wants to protect her daughters from any such bad ideas, reasoning that free speech and an uncensored environment is not always worth the price of the harm done when bad ideas are allowed to spread unchecked. Linda may be correct to think that ideas can do harm and that free speech and a lack of censorship gives bad ideas the chance to spread, but she is still wrong to censor her children's environment and to decide for them how to assess ideas. Writing at the *Edge Foundation*, Mike Godwin has pointed out that:

> "*Dawkins' concept of the meme - ... - forces us to abandon any defense of free speech based on the principle that 'words can never hurt you' ... instead we must defend freedom of expression even though it sometimes allows the spread of 'harmful' ideas, because freedom is the only environment that consistently promotes the discovery or creation of the 'beneficial' ones.*"
> (Mike Godwin; *The Reality Club: The Value of Memes: A Powerful Paradigm or a Poor Metaphor?* at:
> www.edge.org/discourse/memes_thread.html 12.20.96)

Memes are variable - good, bad and ugly. We will carry many memes unwittingly, but that does not stop us from rebelling, from choosing to decide which memes will inform our parenting and which will damage the process. Neither does it give us the right to stop our children from encountering bad ideas. They, like us, need to have access to the full range of ideas in order to be able to discriminate and make rational and creative judgements.

The trick to deciding for ourselves which memes are good or harmful in the arena of parenting is, I want to suggest in the rest of this book, by using our rationality and creativity in a process of conjecture and refutation. It is by asking 'cui bono?' 'Who benefits?' By taking our children seriously, by living in a consensual way with our children so that everyone benefits, everyone wins. Everyone's autonomy is respected when we can best make distinctions between helpful and harmful memes.

Chapter four

Non-coercion and the growth of knowledge

Non-coercive parenting assumes that real learning is intrinsic learning and must, therefore, be based around satisfying preferences.

Replacing coercion with knowledge

When we choose coercion over finding a common preference, we not only lose the possibility of new knowledge being created, but also risk impairing our ability to think, learn, and solve problems. In situations where there is a problem to be solved, coerced children will abandon the attempt to problem solve creatively, knowing it to be futile, since ultimately the solution will be imposed by the adults. Learning does not take place and creativity is trampled.

Children need to have successful experiences of finding solutions and having control over their own lives. Coercion replaces this experience with feelings of powerlessness, resentment, and frustration, adding painful feelings to areas of thinking and another blockage to rational thinking. Coercion helps to convince children that life is difficult, that getting what one wants is next to impossible and that doing things one hates in inevitable. Non-coercion creates flexible thinkers who see that they can control their lives and develop lives that they want to live.

Humans are born to learn. Intrinsic learning and coercion are inimical. TCS parents are in the business of helping their children to satisfy their preferences and pursue their intrinsically motivated learning in every direction. Coercive parents, on the other hand, have a fixed idea of what learning they want their children to do. This agenda sabotages attempts to pursue learning that is not parentally sanctioned. If learning is categorised as 'appropriate' or 'inappropriate', children will either abandon their attempts to have their preferences taken seriously or develop a range of sophisticated coping strategies. Their original preferences can get lost in a maze of subterfuge. They can become adults who are scarcely aware of what their preferences for their own lives are; who are almost certainly convinced that even if they know what they want, they cannot have it.

One of the indicators of coercion damage is the prevalence of entrenched theories. These are theories which are held intransigently and which seem impervious to rational discussion or change. They severely limit the growth of knowledge and sabotage mutually agreed solutions in family life. A regular question from people new to TCS concerns what to do in the face of children who refuse to take part in problem solving. This is a difficult and fraught area for someone who is trying to make a radical switch in their parenting style. It can help to remember that adding more coercion to an already damaged situation is not going to help the situation improve. It is unlikely that parents will find their children unwilling to engage in problem solving in any area at all, so it might be helpful to back away from difficult areas and highlight the progress and success that the family is making in other areas. As children come to trust the process and to see that common preferences can be found, they are more likely to be willing to begin seeking creative solutions in more and more areas of their life.

In many cases, however, the problem is the other way round. Children often find the process of common preferences one that they can adopt very quickly, whilst the parent finds that, despite his or her best efforts, there are certain areas in which they can hardly bear to think about non-coercion.

Getting support from other people who have encountered similar blocks can be very helpful. Sometimes the parent simply needs to back off from the specific area and allow the theory and practice of non-coercion to become more deeply ingrained in his or her lifestyle before s/he can approach the issue again. Most people find that, as they go on living in this radical new paradigm, deeper and deeper areas of entrenched thinking will surface to be dealt with. There begins a lifelong process of moving from entrenched to open thinking.

Theorising about our children

We all, adults and children alike, have areas in which our thinking is damaged by coercion, where we act irrationally or our theories are entrenched. This knowledge can tempt parents to discount certain theories which their children propose, on the basis that they are only saying x or only proposing to act in y way because they are coercion damaged and irrational. This is a dangerous trap to fall into. Attempting to trace in detail the effects of coercion damage or to precisely define or label areas of irrationality is likely to impede our non-coercive dealings with children, and to belittle them rather than take them seriously.

The tendency to make theories about our children is one of the easiest errors to fall into. A distant aunt or enquiring stranger might, in casual conversation, expect that we will be able to rattle off a list of our children's defining attributes in order to fix them in their mind: 'Jane is a tomboy', 'Alan is rather hyperactive', 'Joe has reading difficulties', 'Louise is a maths genius'. The trouble with these theories is that they define the child as a static product, implying that this is what or who the child is and ever shall be. Furthermore, they fix the child according to someone else's outside observations and subjective perceptions. The person, often a parent, might spend a lot of time with the child, be very engaged with the child and know the child well by any conventional measure. Even so, there is still an overlay of theory that is always external and open to being faulty.

The problem for parents is that in order to help our children get what they want, we feel it will assist us if we know what kind of person it is that we are helping. Are we not more likely to make appropriate suggestions that our children will prefer if we have a handy thumb-nail picture of John? Children are individuals. If we begin to treat someone according to a packaged personality type, we are not treating them as a unique and constantly changing individual, but with the gross disrespect of someone who really cannot be bothered to attend to that unique person in the moment. I am not saying that we can know nothing about our children, or that we must begin every engagement as though we were starting from scratch. That would waste time and knowledge. What we must be aware of, though, is the kind of knowledge we have and how best to use it.

We constantly make observations about one another. These observations are fine as long as we do not fall into the trap of having a fixed idea about what Jane will do or want on every future occasion. We should not, for example, start channelling Jane down pre-set routes that fit in with our perceptions and observations.

Rather, we should be tentative about the suggestions we make based on our observations. We do not let our observations become fixed theories. No matter how much time we spend together, we never know what is going on inside someone else's head. Our observations can only ever be of a tiny portion of the learning and thinking and developing within Jane. Once we step back and admit that we are all subjective observers who are fallible and liable to employ our own overlay of perceptions, then we can become more tentative about how we employ our observations and less likely to do damage with them.

Consider Jason, an eleven-year-old who does not exhibit fluent literacy to the observing world. His parents also observe that Jason has a lot of energy and appears (to them) to be often frustrated and destructive. In many conventional homes, Jason would be only a hair's breadth away from being diagnosed with ADHD, medicated with ritalin, labelled as having a specific learning difficulty and plugged into a remedial reading programme. Theorising about Jason leads to seeing him not as a unique person, but as a certain category of child for whom a certain package of solutions can be prescribed. These labels will fix Jason and this 'fixing' will derail his own intrinsic learning processes.

Instead of theorising about our children:
- Acknowledge that our observations are tentative and subjective.
- Be open to refutation or revision.
- Do not waste time and energy trying to get inside a child's mind. Concentrate on solving the present problem and finding out what the child wants. 'I might be wrong, but I got the idea you wanted to get into that book and had a bit of difficulty. Can I help?' 'You don't seem to like being woken up in the mornings, can we find a better way of starting the day that works for you?'
- Remember that the growth of knowledge is not assisted by attempting to second-guess which areas of our children's thinking are damaged and irrational.

Reason and the growth of knowledge

So how does knowledge grow? It grows through reason, through conjecture and refutation. Unfortunately, for many people, that can suggest a very narrow way of working which excludes our emotions and intuition. This does not have to be the case. Just as 'theories' are defined very widely to include such things as personality, assumptions, desires, psychological characteristic, unconscious theories, inexplicit theories and even the inborn theories inherited in our DNA (see chapter 1 above), so reason can also encompass emotion and intuition. In fact all ways of problem solving, explicit and implicit, are part of our reason. The conclusions we reach - whether from logic, feeling, intuition or any other means - still need to be subjected to the process of conjecture and refutation. Knowledge grows when we hold it tentatively and critically, when we are committed to seeking the truth with a constant eye on our own fallibility.

As issues or problems arise within a family, the process adopted is one of finding truth and new knowledge in that situation. This is found through reasoning in the widest sense. A solution is found when all the participants prefer a particular proposal, regardless of how it arose. It is a common preference. The solution does not have to be permanent, it is not absolute truth, but it is held until a new problem arises which requires new knowledge. We reach a new conjecture, something that appears to be true to the best of our knowledge and reasoning, until we encounter some criticism that suggests otherwise and leads us to begin the process again.

Let us take the example of Gillian. Gillian is a first-time mother who, faced with her longed-for baby, suddenly feels confused and overwhelmed. She has planned to breastfeed and intended to share her bed with her baby. Faced with the reality of the totally dependent infant, she finds herself feeling angry when he cries for attention or seems to want to be held constantly. She has a longing for her own personal space, which she has not felt before. She also feels adrift, as though she has no patterns for what mothering might mean for her. Her partner is supportive and helpful and has no strong feelings about Gillian having to breastfeed. Gillian wants to live consensually with her baby and she feels that the baby's unhindered preference would be for breastfeeding, but she also realises that her self-sacrifice would not be good for the baby any more than for herself. Gillian does not believe that she is thinking very clearly, but she has very strong feelings. She feels strongly that she wants to breast-feed. She also feels strongly that she wants to buy some bottles and not have to be the baby's source of nourishment. One friend tells her that to go on breast-feeding would be self-sacrifice and she should stop now before it becomes the chronic pattern of the relationship with her baby. Gillian does not know what to say to her friend, but feels intuitively that this is not quite the case. What she wants is to be able to breast-feed and not feel that she is self-sacrificing. By following this half-articulated intuition, Gillian is subjecting her theories about what is self-sacrifice and what it means to nurture a baby to criticism and refutation. The criticism may not be of the most logical nature, but Gillian's perceptions begin to change. She begins to feel that this nurturing is not a cost or a drain or a sacrifice, but a joy and a preference. Gillian has created new knowledge.

Knowledge grows when it is intrinsic to the learner. Extrinsic motivation is ruled out as an effective strategy for learning and, instead, problem solving is at the heart of learning.

Self-interest and the growth of knowledge

For knowledge to grow, self-interest functions as both an educational principle and a proper foundation for parenting. We are not accustomed to thinking about parenting in terms of facilitating wants, but more as being about controlling wants and behaviour. The conventional assumption is that children are born uncivilised, even wicked, and that their wants will inevitably be bad for themselves and for others, at least for a significant amount of the time, unless they are reigned in.

Consent-based parenting assumes that being 'self-centred' and doing the moral thing co-exist. The goal of parenting is not to control, but to facilitate the child in self-maximising and following their intrinsic motivation. This goal relies on the assumptions that children are rational, creative, trustworthy and autonomous human beings living in environments where they have sufficient information to be able to make good decisions for themselves, by their own lights.

Self-interest is, in fact, the only way to guarantee that those activities engaged in and decisions made are the right ones for any particular individual's learning, growth and well-being. If children rely on parental perceptions of what is right for them, there is actually no way of guaranteeing that the individual child's unique self will be best served. This is because the parents are likely to be working on a preconceived agenda of what is best for children in general or from their own perceptions of the child, which, whilst they might be good approximations, can never be equal to the child's self-knowledge. Children whose intrinsic motivations are being followed and whose self-interest is being helped and facilitated will experience a greater satisfaction from life, a greater belief in their own ability to control their lives and an increase in well-being and self-motivation.

Self-interest is also the optimal way for children to expend their personal resources, as they will do so only so long as they experience benefits. No matter how well a parent knows a child and no matter how well meaning we are as parents, we can never get inside our children's minds. Parents acting out of what they perceive to be a child's best interests will expend resources less optimally, either giving too much or too little in any particular area. Parents do much better to stay within the role of trusted advisor; offering information, best theories and criticism without presuming that in the final analysis they can know best for another person.

Parents are often concerned that if they concede that their children should act out of self-interest, they will be encouraging their children to become monsters who act immorally and with no regard for other people. Acting out of self-interest is often feared as being tantamount to acting badly - a license for abusive behaviour. This is neither what is meant by the theory nor what is experienced in practice. Doing the most optimal thing for one's own self-interest includes doing the right thing. Where it appears to someone that this is not the case, then it is reason and not coercion that is our best tool in convincing the protagonist otherwise. We cannot, ultimately, force someone to lead a moral life, but we can rationally convince children that a moral life and a self-interested life are mutually inclusive because the argument will stand up for itself. Immoral acts tend towards not only harming others, but also to being self-destruction on some level. It is arguable that harming others is not in anyone's self-interest because it involves giving up one's rights to expect respect and serious treatment in return.

By the same token, acts of generosity and service can be acts of self-interest without any contradiction. An aid worker in a famine may give up the prospect of home comforts and put herself into a situation of danger from a desire to effect change and live an altruistic life. Unless she is living her life based on notions of self-destructive irrationality, she will experience job satisfactions that are in line with her own self-interest.

Parents have no good reason to fear self-interest or to juxtapose it against morality. Within a family, of course, there will be a collection of self-interested individuals. It is often assumed that one person following their self-interest will inevitably lead to others having to surrender their self-interest. It is a common, but false, characterisation of TCS that it will be the parents who are the losers in non-coercive households. This is not the case! In chapter six, we will explore some reasons why maximising self-interest is quite compatible with finding common preferences in which everyone wins.

In short:

- Coercion damages learning.
- Theorising about our children and then acting on these theories, even when we believe that we are acting in their best interests, puts serious limits around their learning and growth.
- Our children's knowledge and well-being grows not from force or extrinsic motivation, but from the use of reason and intrinsic motivation.

Self-interest includes doing the right thing.

Part 2:

Putting the theory into practice

Taking Children Seriously gives the theoretical framework for non-coercive consensual relationships between parents and children. Solutions are as diverse as the families seeking them and as unlimited as the creativity available. There is always a solution, even when we do not happen to find one. We may get things wrong, but we can think again. We can afford to be optimistic. In the remaining chapters I want to explore what some of that optimism might look like.

Chapter five

Making the shift

A few fortunate people discover TCS before or very soon after becoming parents, and set out on this adventure from the outset. Most of us discover TCS some way down the line, often after consuming endless parenting manuals and experimenting with every form of conventional parenting. TCS demands a radical paradigm shift, whether we have previously been liberal practitioners of attachment parenting or advocates of strict discipline. The process of entering that paradigm and making the changes to family life can be a daunting period. How to begin? Part of the answer is being able to see just how different TCS is from any other theory of parenting and education.

Discerning the difference from conventional parenting

Those who come to TCS from a relatively liberal perspective often assume that they are simply moving slightly further down an already radical spectrum of parenting. This is not the case. *Taking Children Seriously* demands a major paradigm shift from any previously held parenting theories. Realising this is an important first step.

From authority to fallibilism

Conventional parenting exists on a spectrum from strongly disciplinarian to liberal to laissez-faire parenting. Wherever conventional parents locate themselves along that spectrum, there is always a concept of authority and control at work. This is most obvious with disciplinarian approaches to parenting. Within such philosophies, 'love' and the 'best interests' of the child are often cited as the motivating factors in applying discipline, including corporal discipline. Thus Revd. Carl Haak maintains,

> *"Those children, to whom we give our affection and whom we love so dearly, are sinners, worthy of everlasting hell from the moment they are conceived."*
> (Quotes from www.rsglh.org.parental.discipline.html)

Haak is part of a large tradition of parenting, perhaps best epitomised by Dr. James Dobson, which fears that, without strong correction, their children will be not simply spoilt, but damned. It is an argument from the child's best interests of the highest magnitude and with large stakes. The parent is the authority figure next in line only to God.

Such appeals to authority, however, are not reserved only for those who see themselves as delivering a religious duty to compel obedience. Those who want to take a 'common sense' approach still ultimately appeal to parental authority. There may be family meetings to decide on rules, but it is always the parents who set the parameters and who enforce 'appropriate consequences' when there is an infringement of the 'contracts' agreed to on the basis of parentally controlled choices. Thus one common sense advocate advises,

> *"Present some choices, and ask for his opinions; even if*
> *ultimately you make the decision, he will feel that you respect*
> *his ideas."*   (www.parenting.org)

For those who do not locate authority in a punitive notion of God, but who want to appeal to more than the common sense authority of parents as bearers of wisdom and experience, 'nature' becomes a useful tool. Jean Liedloff, author of *The Continuum Concept*, advises that children are responded to, but should never be the centre of attention. In this life apprenticeship Liedloff observes that very young children soon develop a strong sense of adult expectation and are obedient, quiet or even silent in adult company, conforming totally to the prevailing culture.

Being allowed to develop naturally can sound so like being free to develop autonomously, but the two are not the same. Natural development is actually strictly controlled according to a preordained agenda of what it means to be 'natural', whereas autonomy has no agenda.

Within this style, trust and empathy are encouraged, and guidance and example replace heavy discipline. Misbehaviour is redirected by means of natural and logical consequences and setting of expectations, (see, for example, www.attachmentparenting.org). It all sounds very reasonable, but it retains what every other conventional parenting theory has - an external authority, this time in the guise of nature itself. Almost all conventional parenting styles involve following some extrinsic authority, (with the possible exception being laissez-faire or permissive parenting, which contains other errors). Only consent-based parenting inherently rejects the appeal to unquestioned authority, whether it is a particular religious characterisation of authority, the so-called 'common sense' authority of adults over children, or the authority of nature. The notion that we speak authoritatively by virtue of being parents, even parents who wish to appeal to God or nature, is inimical to the thorough acceptance of our own fallibility and to the pursuit of truth through rationality and creativity. We have to let go of any such opinion before we can make the required paradigm shift. We cannot take children seriously if we are ultimately going to appeal to some extrinsic authority.

Hearing what children say is not enough

Merely listening to children, whether to take account of their views or to negotiate compromises, is a feature of much conventional parenting theory, (particularly, a tenet of liberal parenting), that can be hard to let go of. Listening and negotiating are very good things. They provide key elements in reaching common preferences, but they are not, of themselves, substitutes for common preferences. This is where a paradigm shift is needed. Being 'heard' is no substitute for having a solution that the child actually wants. The goal of TCS is that everyone, children and adults alike, should be genuinely happy with the agreed solution. Merely listening to a child, whether through adult emotions or the child's own words or emotions, does not promise any such solution. Common sense and democratic forms of parenting certainly take children into consideration. They allow that sometimes the child will win. They will also tend to suggest that life is a matter of constant compromise and that learning to give way graciously is both character building and a useful life skill. Many people certainly do go through life believing that they are trapped, that they cannot achieve what they want or ever fully pursue their own happiness. Many people do go through life with fixed theories that they feel chronically unable to change. Many people go through life obviously believing that what they want is of secondary importance. Do we really want our children to be amongst those people?

Winning, without harming others, is possible. Reaching mutual common preferences rather than being heard but overruled by second-best compromises is attainable in families. Self-sacrifice is not the basis of a life well lived, nor is it the essential prerequisite of a generous character. Listening to our children and hearing their emotions without finding solutions which they actually prefer, or inviting our children to negotiate within closed frameworks of already pre-ordained choices, are not enough to foster the rationality, creativity, autonomy and moral family relationships which TCS aspires to.

The myth of best interests

All parenting has the child's best interests at heart, unless it is deliberately abusive. Another key to making the shift to TCS is in ceasing to maintain that best interests can be in any way extrinsically defined. That is not to say that the parent does not have an enormous role in giving advice, best theories and information, but, in the final analysis, best interest must be an intrinsic question of autonomy.

No conventional parenting theory allows for this kind of integrity of autonomy. This is the case even for permissive and laissez-faire parenting, which, by abdicating the parental role of trusted advisor, coerces children with a lack of genuine information from which to make the best choices. It is not for the parent to decide that it is in the child's best interest to receive the so-called discipline of God, or to follow what everyone agrees on as 'common sense', or to live a life without sugar, plastic toys, or TV as so-called 'nature' intended. These are decisions for the child. The parent may have theories about religion or received wisdom or sweets that should be shared as fully as the child desires; but imposition of those theories, even those theories that the parent is quite convinced are correct and true, is not an option.

Why not? Firstly, because no matter how convinced the parent is, they could still be wrong. Secondly, because no matter how well a parent knows their child, and no matter how much they love their child, they are not their child.

Love is not an excuse

A child is a separate person with a moral right to his or her own autonomy. Love is not a good enough excuse for acting immorally to deliberately compromise that autonomy. The idea of loving coercion is pernicious, and runs through every strand of conventional parenting. Laissez-faire and permissive parents inflict coercive neglect in the name of love. Religious fundamentalists and other authoritarian parents inflict discipline, from spanking, to time out to loss of privileges, in the name of love. Liberal parents seek to impose firm but loving limits. TCS completely eschews the idea that coercion of any kind, no matter how subtly conceived and implemented, can be an act of love.

Conventional parents, by and large, do love their children. TCS parents do not have the monopoly on love any more than they do on infallibility. The point is simply that a big shift in perception is needed for TCS parenting to take place, a shift away from the dogma that love justifies coercion of any form.

With no outcomes in mind

Another switch that characterises the paradigm shift between conventional and TCS parenting is the movement away from predicting or prescribing outcomes for our children. Authoritarian parents tend to have very clear pictures of the kinds of people they want and expect their children to become. The ideal is likely to include attributes like godliness, respect for authority, selflessness, industriousness, and so on. Laissez-faire parents, on the other hand, may have hopes for revolutionary free-thinkers and independence. Those between these extremes, particularly those following democratic liberal styles of parenting, may have more amorphous aims in mind. Deborah Critzer, for example proposes that a childhood of *"respect, nurture and loving guidance"* will result in *"rounded, responsible, successful adults"* (see www. positiveparenting.com). TCS does not make any such predictions or encourage any kind of searching for outcomes in our children.

The conventional assumption is that children are products, and a product, as we all know, has to meet certain standards and criteria before it can be acceptable. For conventional parenting, this often means that children who do not meet the required specification are labelled. The labelling might be judgmental and intended to shame: 'Harry is a naughty child'; 'Becky is such a wilful, stubborn little girl'; 'Katie is a selfish little so and so'. Alternatively, it might be the kind of labelling which categorises children according to the growing plethora of 'syndromes'. Labelling neatly accounts for their faultiness without ever needing to question whether they are simply distressed human beings who are not resilient to all the coercion in their lives.

Imagine a busy school classroom. In an ethos where the product mentality is operating, a child who waits until everyone has got started on the work the group has been instructed to do before asking, *"And what should I do?"* attracts a host of 'faulty product' labels. Options are worked through. Is the child 'deaf'? Should the child be seen as 'deliberately annoying' and brought up to specification with behavioural management strategies? Should the child be seen as 'slow'? Should the child be given a useful label such as 'Asperger's syndrome' or 'ADHD', so that support, behavioural modification, and medication can all be brought to bear?

The product mentality of conventional parenting allows parents to long for their particular definition of a child masterpiece and encourages them to feel disappointed or even deliberately thwarted when this is not what they get. Most parents will agree that their child is unique. Yet conventional parenting also assists parents in attaching labels to their children that diminish the humanity of children who dare to display their individuality.

Simply thinking about our children in this demeaning way distorts the relationship and tends to exacerbate a whole range of subtle coercion. What we see of another person is only what is visible at that time. It is a small snapshot of a process, not a static definition. In a lifetime, we are lucky if we come to understand ourselves well. It is presumptuous and demeaning to think that we can know another.

If our children are not products, then what does it matter that at any one moment a child is consumed with a particular subject to the exclusion of everything else or does not seem to be as social as her peers? We make observations, always partial, though sometimes helpful. There is nothing wrong with offering up observations that might help our children – 'If you don't look at people when you're talking, you might find that they think you're lying'. It is, however, not reasonable, helpful, or necessary to coerce a child into making eye contact by placing him in some behavioural modification programme or by constantly barraging him with information that he has long since tired of hearing. The point is to help the individual child live his own life by his own lights in the way that most pleases him, not to mould him into a new set of attributes which seem more functional and pleasing to parents who want a higher level of product satisfaction. This is true, even when the moulding is dressed up in the insidious cloak of being for the child's 'own good'.

The only question that remains is, 'How can I help my child do the things he wants with his life?' Children need to be free from being seen as products or from being objectified and defined by a list of subjective observations. They need parents who are unquestioningly on their side, not to impose their own or so-called expert agendas on their children in the name of loving assistance, but simply to assist their children in carrying forward their own intrinsically motivated lives in process.

The myth of natural consequences

Conventional parenting tends to elevate certain bad things happening to the status of being 'natural' or 'logical', by which is meant 'inevitable'. This is done in order to manipulate children's behaviour without parents ever having to take responsibility for this gross manipulation. 'If you don't eat up your breakfast, you will suffer from hunger'; 'If you climb in that tree, you will fall and hurt yourself'; 'If you run around the house, you will cause an accident'; 'If you don't go to sleep at a reasonable hour, you will make yourself ill', and so on. The parent makes it look as though the bad thing that is going to happen simply has to happen, but this is just not true. There are lots of different things that might happen if you avoid breakfast, like having a snack later, or finding that you are the sort of person who does not particularly miss this meal. Hunger will only result if the child is refused any food two hours later. This is not a natural consequence, but a parentally decided-upon consequence meant to teach the child a lesson. It is nothing more than a cruel and coercive deceit to say, 'I told you so', **and** claim that the consequence is nothing to do with the parent.

There are times when bad things happen despite our best efforts to prevent them, but TCS parents can go a long way to minimise such times. They can give lots of information about nutrition and body clocks and individual patterns of eating and how to get access to food at lots of different times. They can discuss the safest ways of climbing and the best kind of trees to use and find out about other climbing opportunities to extend these skills. They can ensure that children can sleep when it suits them and do not have to be artificially and coercively either woken or forced to sleep.

The cry often comes back from conventional parents, 'But how will he ever learn about...?'. The simple answer is that children will learn through information and discussion. Children do not have to experience artificial consequences dressed up as 'natural' in order to learn the laws of physics or how their bodies work or what people's attitudes to different sorts of behaviour might be. Children are not going to learn how to think rationally and creatively about problems and how to overcome them by being fed a diet of lies about what will happen to them if they try out certain things. If there is a good reason why a child should not do something, then the reason should be able to stand for itself and not need the back up of made-up 'consequences'. If the reason not to do something does not stand up to scrutiny, it should be revised, not propped up by coercion in the garb of 'nature' or 'common sense'.

Summarising the paradigm shift

The shift from conventional to TCS parenting is an enormous leap of perception and lifestyle, but we can do a great deal to assist ourselves in making the leap:

- Give up any allegiance to imposing extrinsic authority.
- Recognise our own fallibility at all times.
- Do not simply listen to and hear our children, but actively work with them to find mutually preferable solutions.
- Give advice, but desist from insisting that we know what is best for another autonomous human being.
- Beware of using love as a motive for coercion.
- Do not prescribe the product that your child should be.
- Do not dress artificial consequences in the guise of natural consequences, but use your parental role to alleviate consequences with information and assistance.

Once we have made this paradigm shift, our lives will never be the same again. We will find ourselves facing new challenges in parenting, some of which may be particularly acute in the early stages of making the shift, but will lead to a life of learning and winning for all your family.

Avoiding self-sacrifice

So, you have made the paradigm shift and are eager to start parenting in a new and consensual way. The aim is to build consent via common preferences, but for parents who are new to this way of thinking, it often seems much easier to fall into self-sacrifice. We desperately want to stop coercing, but we are not used to the kind of creative problem-solving that achieves common preferences. In an attempt to avoid coercion at all costs, we short circuit the entire creative problem-solving process and just give in. Of course, it does not really help. Few of us can sustain self-sacrifice without building up stores of resentment that are likely to erupt in coercion at some point, either in a massive blow out or in a steady, corrosive stream of coercive remarks or subtle manipulations. Furthermore, we are denying our children access to the very creativity and rationality that is at the core of TCS and which makes it so much more than merely non-coercive parenting.

When all our rationality and creativity fails - as it sometimes will, given our fallibility - it is better for a parent to self-sacrifice than to coerce. This is an extreme default, however, used in failure and as little as possible. It is not a recommendation or a normal way of relating to our children. That said, self-sacrifice happens, because we are fallible. It is likely to happen more frequently when we are just making the transition to a new paradigm and have few models of common preferences to draw on. Most parenting theories, after all, have some concept of how noble it is to sacrifice ourselves for our children, so it is an easy mode to slip into.

How do we know when we are self-sacrificing and what can we do about it? We know that we are in a state of self-sacrifice when:
- We never actually prefer the outcome of any given problem-solving attempt.
- We begin to think that it is inevitable that parents should feel like martyrs.
- We are telling ourselves that we must lose in order for our children to win.
- We sense that the whole situation is volatile, guilt ridden, and liable to an ugly melt down at any moment.
- We feel resentful or burnt out or both.

Parents who continually self-sacrifice are not giving their children any example of problem-solving or getting the best from life in the long term. Rather, they are presenting a skewed picture of childhood as the time for satisfaction, before the child grows up in the real world of becoming a long-suffering doormat. This does our children a tremendous disservice. It deprives them of a lifelong model of positive and consensual problem-solving. It gives them so little to look forward to, they can hardly be blamed if they become grasping and uncaring while they have the limited chance as children. Whilst the children of self-sacrificing parents become ever more insistent and demanding that their needs and wants are met this minute and without question, the parents themselves are likely to become more and more depressed and resentful and ever less creative.

We can only begin to break this cycle when we convince ourselves that life does not have to be like this. If we believe that self-sacrifice is not noble but actually draining and harmful, then we are more likely to resist it. If we are convinced that there are solutions out there, even when we fail to find them, then we are more likely to start again positively. If we are convinced that each scenario does not require that some lose whilst others win, that we can in fact build consent into our family relationships, then we will not be satisfied with self-sacrifice. Instead, we will reserve self-sacrifice only as that infrequent moral default when all else fails us.

Consent is optimum when everyone in the family, adults and children alike, take themselves seriously, and each expects to live the life that they truly prefer within the family group. When this is happening, adults and children can all be open to changing their preferences without ever fearing that it will mean doing something they really do not want to do. This releases an enormous flood of creativity for solving problems consensually. To stop self-sacrificing, we need to think seriously about what it is that we want. This does not mean that we have to become intransigent or unable to revise our theories. We should start from what we want, not from what we do not want. We should believe that we could get what we want, and communicate to our children that we can get what we want without in any way needing to coerce them. Children who are used to self-sacrificing parents may be sceptical about this, but they will soon come to trust the process if they see that everyone can win, and that their parent's new found seriousness about their own needs is not going to be at the children's expense. In the longer term, children will be very happy to have a creative model of finding common preferences, which they know will serve them in continuing to get what they want as they move into adulthood. The future will look as flexible and full of possibility as the present.

Building the win-win mentality

The key to avoiding self-sacrifice is in building a win-win mentality. This is something that conventional parenting does not prepare us for. Few of us believe that everyone can win. We are schooled to accept that only some can win, that we must compromise, that we have to take turns at getting what we want. TCS proposes that we think like this because we fail to use our resources of creativity and rationality. If we determine to work together to find common preferences, it can be done; the more we do it, the more creative we get and the more new knowledge we generate.

Being able to do this rests on the separation of two important theories. The first is that we are fallible. Since we are fallible, we will make mistakes and we will sometimes fail to find solutions. At any given time, we can work only with the knowledge and theories that we have at that moment. These may sometimes be inadequate to the situation, resulting in a dead end, self-sacrifice, or even coercion.

The second theory is crucial, however, if we are not to give up: there is always a solution out there. We may fail to find solutions because of our fallibility and limited knowledge at any one moment, but this is not the same as believing that no solution was even theoretically possible. There was a solution, probably several solutions, but we simply did not find it on this occasion. The self-sacrificing or coercive parent may be willing to acknowledge some level of fallibility (though children are usually characterised as **more** fallible than adults), but they are generally unwilling to admit that a solution could have existed in theory. Rather, they insist that their actions were inevitable, that someone had to lose. TCS proposes a very different fundamental premise, namely that solutions always exist, at least in theory, whether or not we manage to find them in any given situation. TCS parents believe that this premise is yet to be falsified, and in practice it gives them an essential basis for building the win-win mentality.

Let us consider the Jones family, which has three children aged 18, 14 and 12. Mum Jones has heard about TCS and thinks it might be for them, but has lots of questions. Dad Jones thinks it is mad. Sally (18) thinks it is OK for older teenagers, but surely the younger ones **need** coercion to keep them in line. Joanne and Peter think it sounds great, but they are sceptical too - they still think Mum will coerce them when the chips are down.

Today is a busy day. Dad has a pile of work he wants to get through. Sally is leaving for an important holiday with friends and wants a lift to the airport. Joanne really wants to see a certain friend today, who lives some distance away from the city so there is no public transport. Sally and Joanne have already had a row. Sally thinks Joanne's trip is unimportant as she could go any time and Mum should take Sally to the airport instead of Joanne to the friend's house. Joanne thinks Sally always gets everything her way

- she has not seen her friend in ages and there is a bus straight to the airport. Peter wants to go to a park today, as he has been practicing some new stunts on his skateboard and wants to do some more. He also wants pizza for lunch. Mum wants to get through the day sane and hopes for a cup of coffee (with caffeine!) at some point. Dad says it is nothing to do with him, he has to earn a living and, by the way, 'I told you you couldn't all get what you want.'

The best scenarios are going to occur when everyone in the family subscribes to TCS, but even here there are possible solutions. We have to remember that solutions ultimately have to be the ones that particular people prefer. Knowing that a solution is theoretically possible does not always give us the creativity to find it, but it does make us look at things differently. It is an enormous mind-shift that has a real effect. We also have to remember that the final solution may not look anything like the initial problem(s). The art of finding common preferences is the art of creativity and openess. We can change our preferences; something better can come along at any moment.

Any number of things could happen. Dad might be persuaded to take just a long enough break to take Sally to the airport, freeing up Mum to drive with Joanne and Peter to Jo's friend's, pick up the friend, and take them all to a pizza restaurant near a park. The girls could have time together and Peter could skateboard. Mum could get two cappuccinos at the restaurant and read half a novel in the park.

Dad might be totally intransigent and remain outside of the loop. Mum, having talked some more to the children, might realise that there is a new movie opening today that Jo and Peter both want to see. She could drop them at the cinema on the way to the airport. Before setting out, she could ring the mother of Jo's friend, who might agree to bring her daughter for an overnight stay later that day. Then, after the friend arrives, Mum and Peter could head for the park via McDonalds (Peter having changed that preference) and Mum could relax in the park café with delicious real coffee and cakes.

Dad may remain fixed, but Mum finds that Jo and Peter would rather go bowling than go to a friend's or to the park, so she drops them on the way to taking Sally to the airport and joins them there later for her coffee.

Alternatively, Dad stops being a grump, and realises that he has a client he could visit who lives close by Jo's friend. He could take her and still be working, and he would prefer that to the office. Mum will take Sally to the airport, then have an afternoon to herself in the city. Peter is happy to stay home - with Dad out of the office, he can have access to the computer without interruption. Or something else entirely different could happen ...

The point is that there is not some fixed, pre-determined solution out there that has to be mystically divined, nor is it that there are no solutions and someone has to suffer. Rather, we can build consensual 'win-win' families if we start by believing that solutions are always theoretically possible. Solutions are as practical and available as our own creativity. What prevents us finding solutions is not that they cannot exist, but that we are fallible.

Learning from mistakes

Owning and recognising our fallibility does not mean that we have to get stuck on it. We make mistakes. These mistakes need not lead us to despair, but can be used as opportunities for learning and growth. Conventional wisdom tells us that mistakes are bad and that guilt will follow. Conventional parenting seems to have two main responses to parental mistakes. The first is to wallow in guilt, feeling that we can never get it right, endlessly agonising and mentally beating ourselves up for not being able to do it all, be it all, and self-sacrifice with a smile. The second is to claim that we can only do what we can do, that we can only be 'good enough'. This must inevitably mean that sometimes our children are going to have to lose and get used to the fact that this is what the 'real world' is like.

TCS takes neither of these coercive paths. We make mistakes, but we recognize that agonising and living in guilt just undermines our motivation and traps us in a futile cycle of negativity. We can only act from what we know in the moment, but this neither necessitates nor justifies coercion and immorality. TCS parents own their responsibility towards their children and do not diminish this with weak arguments about inevitability when they fail. At the same time, TCS parents see no need for these failings to be a reason for paroxysms of guilt. We can always apologise when we make mistakes towards our children. We can recognise our responsibility and not merely justify our errors. This done, TCS parents can then rejoice that they have seen the error and can now criticise it, learn from it and move on.

As long as we are alive, we should always be learning. What better way to learn than by a constant process of conjecture, refutation and new knowledge? Being able to say that we were wrong and then move on to develop a new theory are matters for celebration, not guilt. Certainly, there are things we will and should regret, but being able to think about these things clearly and to work out how to change without being burdened by self-loathing is much more likely to effect change that will benefit both parent and children.

Sometimes we do not understand why we make particular mistakes. We may have all sorts of triggers that are hidden deep within our psyche or which arise from ideas that we have imbibed without ever being able to articulate them. We may never fully get to the bottom of such inexplicit theories, but we can learn to notice our triggers. We can spend time thinking about ways to disengage or behave differently when those triggers arise. Our actions are not predetermined. We always have a choice. Knowing this can make it much easier to avoid or recover from even the most ingrained of mistakes.

When we have come to see our mistaken behaviour as something that we can change and use as a springboard for learning, we also start to treat our children's mistakes differently. Children are fallible, too. Conventional parenting often assumes that children do certain things to test their parents, or to deliberately engage in a power struggle over rightful parental boundaries. TCS rejects this kind of thinking, which sets children up as the enemy. Mistakes occur when we lack information or creativity. Children, like adults, have limited knowledge. Mistakes are bound to arise. There is no need to regard these mistakes as a deliberate challenge or the setting out of battle lines.

Question everything

In the final analysis, we make the paradigm shift to TCS most successfully when we are able to question absolutely everything. Why should we all go to sleep at 11p.m. and get up at 7.30 a.m.? Why should parents (or anyone) be seen as figures of authority? Why do we so easily believe that acting immorally towards our children (in the form of coercion) can be justified for some perceived benefit like clean teeth? Why should not our children stay in their pyjamas all day? Why do we think the world will end if our children drink coke or love watching TV? The list is endless. When we start to take our children and ourselves seriously, then real individuals with real preferences and real problems to be solved replace all the received conventional wisdom about how we should think and behave. It is a process in which our whole worldview is likely to be constantly changing. It is both enormously scary and endlessly liberating.

TCS is not simply a slightly more radical form of liberal parenting on a spectrum that we can choose to slide back and forth along. TCS parenting demands a whole paradigm shift to a world of consensual relationships where everything, absolutely everything, can be and will be questioned. It demands that we begin to think differently in order to be able to act differently.

- Do not accept self-sacrifice as the common lot of parents. Watch out for signs of it and deal with them as creatively as you can.
- Do believe that everyone can win - if you do not really think that a solution exists you will not be committed to looking for it.
- Accept that you will make mistakes and so will your children, but do not wallow in guilt or give up - learn from mistakes.
- Question everything.

In this new paradigm, parents, accustomed as we are to fixed solutions, often desperately reach for practical examples of how to live with autonomous children. There can be no definitive answers. Solutions are as various and unique as the individuals involved at any one moment. It is possible, however, to explore scenarios and begin to get a feel for a new and consensual way of working, as I will explore in the next chapter.

Chapter six

Everyone's a winner

How do we build consensual family relationships and find common preferences? To go beyond mere non-coercion to genuinely learning to win requires:

- Relationships in which there are no opposing sides.
- Learning to seek solutions outside the immediate situation by pooling creativity.
- Fostering an environment in which all parties are open to changing their first preferences.
- Accepting that self-interest and common preferences are mutually inclusive.
- Letting go of memes that sabotage our attempts at rationality and creativity, for example, the notion of 'fairness' as it is commonly conceived.

On the same side

Conventional parenting polarises families. On one side there are parents, struggling to retain control and impose rules or limits that are deemed to be in their children's best interests. There is an assumption that, at some level, children and parents are working towards opposite ends, and it is up to the parents to take the reigns and steer the family to the good. This is the case even when the steering comes in the form of sugar-coated 'loving guidance'. On the other side, there are children, constantly testing the boundaries and needing to be taught lessons. Without 'loving discipline', the wisdom runs, they will become selfish, insatiable monsters. The notion of artificial boundaries is at the core of this polarised thinking. It is also aided by the myth that we cannot all win, that there must be compromises and losers.

We need to reject these assumptions. In TCS families, everyone is expected to be on their own side. Each individual knows best what he or she wants and prefers. Far from creating untold conflict, this allows for rational discussion of how all of these interests can be met through common preferences where everyone wins. There is no such thing as doing something in the 'family's best interest' when one or more members of the family are deeply unhappy with the solution.

Being able to create an environment in which everyone wins relies on several things. It is absolutely necessary that children can trust that they can enter into the process of finding a common preference without fear of coercion. It is only when they can do this that they will be able to see that they can change their preferences and still get what they want. Without this trust, they are much more likely to stick rigidly to their first preference, fearing that if they show any open-mindedness on a particular subject they will merely be trampled upon. Similarly, parents must be willing to go into the process without having already decided what the outcome must be. They must be willing not simply to desist from coercion, but also to use all their creativity to find common preferences.

So, parents and children are not working against one another, but are working for consent and **common** preference. What might that look like? Let us imagine the Potter family. The Potters have five children under the age of seven: Jenny (7), Sam (5), Lucy (4), Katie and Rachel (both 2), and baby Ben (3 months). Mum is exhausted. She cannot remember what a preference is, never mind find one. Dad is supportive of mum and TCS, but also exhausted – he is the only earner and things are pushed at work. Ordinary things are starting to get Mum down. The laundry seems to conspire against her. She longs to have a tidy corner of the house, but cannot ever seem to catch up. There are constant running squabbles that never seem to be resolved between the children.

Firstly, it is worth noting that this just is a difficult situation, and introducing coercion would not change that. Screaming does not get laundry done and making one another miserable is not going to help anyone. Mum clearly needs help. Could Dad change his work schedule to make things more flexible? Are there good friends or grandparents or babysitters or other adults who could help? Adding adults or friendly teenagers to this situation could improve things enormously, even if it is only very part-time assistance.

It might be that Jenny, Sam and Lucy (at least), have friends they could go to spend days or parts of days with. Conversely, it might be that the children could invite friends to spend days or parts of days with them in return - they may be a lot happier and play with more contentment when there are **more** children that they especially want to be with. Increasing the number of children, although it might not seem like the obvious solution, could actually help enormously.

Turning to a different part of the problem, a complete de-clutter of the house and re-arrangement of all the storage could make quite an improvement. Mum probably feels too exhausted to do this alone three months after giving birth, but she could hire someone to do this and a thorough clean - a one off payment to set up more helpful ways for the future. Or she may have friends or family who would be prepared to give this kind of help. Perhaps a local teenager would do parts of the cleaning for reasonable rates, or perhaps the teenager would play with some or all of the children for certain periods in return for computer access. On the laundry front, Mum could go to a charity shop, (or several), and buy lots of clothes for the children so that she would only need to do one mammoth laundry session once a week, or this could become a regular and manageable contribution from Dad.

Mum could change her preferences about how tidy the house really needs to be and feel more comfortable in a different environment, or she could think about what are the things that make her most comfortable and just concentrate on those. This might mean reaching a common preference about having a tidy bedroom or a tidy zone around a special chair.

Mum should also enlist the support of the children - 'I want us all to get what we want so I need your ideas all the time and we need to work together to find the things that work best for us'. Tiredness and mistakes are travelling companions, so Mum needs to be ready to see her mistakes and apologise. It also helps if, when the children make mistakes, she can see them as just that - failures of creativity by people who lack practice at trial and error solutions, but who are trying to get better. Mum should not start seeing the children as monsters conspiring to make her miserable. What would be more helpful, would be thinking ahead and planning to have lots of favourite activities available for stressful times. A pile of books for reading to the twins by the favourite chair for feeding the baby; a good selection of videos easily accessible; favourite CD-Roms pre-installed and easy to start; a table with art things out all the time; easily accessible snacks and drinks that the children can help themselves to. These might be life savers in those moments when there seems to be lots of demands all at once.

With so many small children, it will be a good idea to build in extra time for making trips or meeting appointments. Stressful rushes to get ready can easily sour otherwise enjoyable events. Mum may also think of ways to build in escape plans from events or activities that the family soon feel they want to get out of. On other days, some creative thinking might be required to meet different wants. Take a day when everyone except Sam wants to go to a local meeting for home educating families. Is there a friend Sam could spend the day with? Perhaps Jenny and Lucy could go to the home educators' meeting with another family, and Mum could go to the park with the others. That way, Jenny and Lucy get to see their friends, Sam is pleased, the twins are just as happy with the park and baby has an onboard milk supply. There might even be a really good café in the park that Mum loves! Or perhaps everyone would really prefer to go out to a fun fair and buy ice cream. Or the solution might be something else entirely different.

'The Disney Solution'

The important thing is that a solution is found which everyone generally prefers. There are many ways of problem solving, as many as our joint creativity allows. Sometimes a useful way to problem-solve is to take apart the expressed preferences and see what are the elements that are making something a want.

A few weeks before his birthday, for example, 7-year-old Ben announces that he wants a Playstation 2. Money is very tight in the Lewis household and the family have previously heavily invested in setting up PCs for the family with a good range of games. Dad is concerned not only with the initial outlay, which is at least £100 more than they had budgeted for the birthday, but also that there will then be a need to buy games for the new machine, which will not work on the other family machines. After some talking and brainstorming, the family begin to feel stuck and no-one seems to be changing any preference. Then Ben's older sister, Liz, notices what Ben is actually saying about the Playstation. What he wants most of all is not different games, but more control over the way he can play the games. Liz suggests buying a wheel and a control pad to fit onto the family PC. Ben is delighted with the suggestion and happily changes his preferences. Dad is happy to help Ben try out equipment at the local computer store and is happy to extend the budget a bit. After all the family will not have to find money for games that fit only one machine.

We have to be prepared to do a bit of creative deconstructing of preferences; to ask, what is actually wanted here? Sometimes, it is not as obvious as we think. Taking things apart can lead to a good solution. Of course, sometimes that does not happen, and then we may need to try another method of problem solving.

On the *Taking Children Seriously* Internet discussion list, one of these methods of problem solving has become fondly known as 'The Disney Solution'. Jane wants to go ice-skating, Philip wants to go to the movies, Ellie wants to go to the park. No-one seems to be open-minded. Mum says, *"How about a trip to Disneyland instead?"* Suddenly, everyone is in agreement. It does not have to be Disneyland! The point is that most families have a few activities that they really enjoy and which might break an impasse. It might be that the solution needed is something that is not amongst any of the initial preferences, but something entirely different, something that does not have the feel of one person being talked into doing another person's choice but, instead, enables everyone to think outside of the current box.

Creativity and changing preferences

If children trust that they will not be risking coercion by taking part in problem solving, if their creativity is valued and used, then the idea of changing preferences becomes much less threatening. Parents can generally see that the ability of children to change their preferences is a crucial one, but it is much easier to overlook the necessity for adults to change their preferences, too. In chapter one, I looked at how coercion damages our ability to think, and in chapter three at how harmful memes and entrenched theories can inhibit our creativity. This can happen to anyone, at any age, but adults have generally encountered much more coercion damage and are particularly likely to have areas that they find it virtually impossible to discuss rationally and openly. It is worth remembering this when an issue seems particularly hard to think about or change your mind about. Parents, not just children, must be willing to change their preferences, if they are to facilitate consent as the *modus operandi* of their families.

Changing our preferences is not the same as self-sacrifice. If we are looking for genuine consent and common preferences, the changes in our thinking have to be real. If we feel that we are merely compromising, or if we feel resentful or uneasy about solutions, then there is no point in kidding ourselves that we have arrived at a common preference. Changing preferences is not easy, especially in entrenched areas, but the more we commit ourselves to finding consensual solutions and the more we practice finding common preferences, the more it will happen. One thing that we can do to help the process is to ask ourselves if the thing we are expressing a preference about is really an area where we have the right to interfere. I might prefer a tidy house, but does that give me a right to insist that my children should have tidy bedrooms, any more than I would have the right to insist that an adult friend should have a tidy house? I might prefer a vegetarian diet, but does that give me the right to impose a vegetarian diet on my children?

I am not suggesting that these are simple, clear-cut areas. The examples above are complicated by the fact that we have a special relationship with our children, and they might be happy to reach a common preference with us even if we do not have a 'right' to expect this. The examples are also complicated by the practicalities of sharing a home, and by the fact that we have a responsibility as parents to share information and our best theories about hygiene and life-style and diet and anything else. Even with these provisos, however, it can sometimes help us to see things differently if we simply ask ourselves, 'Would I presume to interfere so closely with an adult friend? Is this properly an area where I should be expressing a preference?'

Another way in which we can help ourselves to change preferences is to seek both criticism of our theories and new information. All too often, we live within a milieu in which consensual living is viewed as anything from impossible to dangerous to quirky. Within such a milieu, it is hard to find a wider pool of creativity and criticism to challenge our more coercive or entrenched theories. To some extent, we have to be prepared to do this for ourselves, but there is help available. Children are often willing to act as astute critics. If they trust that it is safe to do so, they will generally be very generous with their criticism, pointing out coercion and presenting cogent reasons why our pet theories might be wrong after all. More widely, there are other people trying to live consensually, and gaining access to their ideas and criticisms can be an invaluable aid in working on entrenched theories. It might be through the regular *Taking Children Seriously* journal, or the more immediate medium of the TCS Internet mailing list, or through building relationships with particular families.

A third way of helping ourselves to change preferences is to ask ourselves what we care about most. Are we really more wedded to an idea that watching more than two hours of TV is bad for a person than we are to our child's happiness? Do we really think that avoiding a glass of cola is more important to our child's well being and thinking, than avoiding massive distress? Changing our preferences is not merely about changing the outward way we behave towards our children, but goes to the core of our inner thoughts and feelings change. *Taking Children Seriously* is not a burdensome code to be slavishly followed and implemented, but a positive choice about how we value one another and want to behave morally and creatively towards one another. Simply reminding ourselves of this can often help us to begin solving problems that seem to have come to an impasse.

At other times, we may simply need more time. A theory may be so entrenched that we are not ready to examine it at all. We will need more practice at finding common preferences in easier areas before we are willing to return and expose this difficult ground. At such times, the best thing we can do is to back off. There are plenty of other problems to be solved.

Self-interest and common preferences

Self-interest is a good and proper thing for a child to exhibit. Likewise, consent-based family relationships with the goal of finding common preferences are desirable and possible. Are these things really compatible? Why should a child who can have what she wants be interested in helping other family members to get what they want? Is not the best we can hope for a compromise that people can live with? Is not the self-interested child going to take up an intransigent stance and repeat his position or demands until they are met, in the full knowledge that he is not going to be coerced?

It is important to stress that common preferences are not compromises. If there is a compromise, then it is likely that someone is feeling coerced and someone's self interest has been disregarded. If a child appears intransigent, then perhaps he is unconvinced that it is safe to let go of his original preference and explore new ideas that might bring him something that he prefers more. Alternatively, he may have already reached a good solution and the criticisms of it are genuinely unconvincing to him. A common preference is reached only when every one of the participants genuinely prefers the solution. If every-one genuinely prefers something, there is no conflict with self-interest. Children are interested in helping the whole family, parents and siblings, to reach such common preferences. They trust that, in the process, they will be fully respected and may very well find something that they prefer over their original suggestion. If a child knows that she will not be coerced, there is no reason to cling to a demand without the possibility of thinking or problem solving. After all, it is quite possible that her first suggestion will end up being preferable to everyone, and if not, she can be confident that the end result will be something even better than she had first suggested.

The myth of fairness

One thing that often stands in the way of finding common preferences is the myth of 'fairness'. Conventional parenting tells us that all children should be treated the same or equally. If we buy six bags of crisps, then each of the three children should consume two bags over the next few days. Most of us were brought up in families where parents and grandparents told us, 'You can't give to one without giving to the other.' Surely, it is common sense that we should treat our children fairly and equally, that we should not discriminate between them? This is not taking children seriously. Children are individuals. If we buy Tim chocolate simply because we bought some for Lizzie, we are not taking any notice of Tim's individuality and real preferences, but rather relating to him by means of a mechanical principle.

The notion of fairness promotes a climate of sibling rivalry in which children are constantly watching one another and their parents for signals of unfairness or favour. Conversely, if we treat each child as an autonomous individual with his or her own preferences which we want to help them achieve, then both fairness and rivalry become superfluous. Lizzie wants chocolate and a movie. Tim wants to spend some time reading with mum and would like pizza for tea. Perhaps all of those things are simply achievable. Perhaps there is some problem. The answer is not to tell Tim, 'Well, today we are all going to the movies. I'll buy you some sweets and I'm sure you'll enjoy it, really. I read to you yesterday. So it's only fair'. The answer is to find a common preference. That may mean that everyone will do the same thing because everyone decides that they had not considered the idea of going bowling and they would all prefer that to their original ideas. It may mean Lizzie will end up going for a bike ride with her friend and stopping off at the sweet shop on her way, whilst Mum and Tim snuggle up with the book and later Dad cooks paella, which everyone prefers to pizza. When we take each child seriously, we have to abandon any allegiance to mechanical rules.

Finding common preferences

So, you want to help your children to find common preferences, but you are as fallible as the next person and come with your own entrenched theories, one of which is likely to be the pervasive idea that most of the time someone has to be disappointed. There are no rules for finding common preferences. What works for one family may be of little use to another, but, in general, common preferences are more likely when:

- We believe that a solution is possible, even if we do not find it.
- The participants believe themselves to be on the same side, rather than seeing themselves as adversaries.
- Everyone can discuss their preferences openly.
- Rationality and creativity are used to tease out the vital elements of a preference that may lead to new solutions.
- Solutions are looked for widely, with the possibility of a Disney solution.
- Participants can risk changing their preferences without fear of coercion.
- Parents acknowledge their children's autonomy and, so, free up areas where they do not need to have preferences about other people's lives, (though they may offer information and advice).
- Parents prefer being on their children's side and helping them to get what they want and avoid distress.
- Creativity and self-interest are fully valued and utilised.
- Concepts such as fairness are abandoned.

Chapter seven

Learning to win

Conventional parenting relies on artificial boundaries; not the type of boundaries that protect our personal privacy and integrity, but the kind of extrinsic limits which adherents claim come from God, common sense, logic, nature or some other external force. These are put forward as fixed, irrefutable points that are viewed as resistant to or more important than non-coercion. Despite this, no two parenting theories will ever totally agree about these boundaries.

We commonly think that rules will keep us safe, but they will not. Rules are mechanical, contrived and extrinsic. When a situation arises in which the rule does not apply sufficiently, or where an exception is needed, or when the extrinsic control is removed and the child is alone to make a decision, rules are often inadequate. Rules cannot substitute for our ability to think and solve problems. We are at our most creative and innovative - not to mention safest - when we are assessing every aspect of a problem or situation to arrive at a solution that is uniquely tailored and appropriate.

The goal of learning to win is not to live by mechanical rules, but to expand our problem solving and thinking. Learning to win demands constant and creative thought, replacing extrinsic controls with conjecture and refutation. Learning to win promotes intrinsic motivation and the constant growth of knowledge that accompanies it. It is about constantly pushing the limits of knowledge and what is possible. Whereas extrinsic controls give us rules to follow in model situations, learning to win fosters autonomy, flexibility and rationality to negotiate real situations, even when the models fail to apply. How do we learn to win, especially in areas where it has previously seemed to be self-evident to us that coercion has to be a necessary feature of parenting?

The age of reason

The notion that children can be given incremental freedom as they get older and become 'more reasonable' is a pervasive one. In particular, babies and toddlers are targeted as the main focus of boundary parenting. There is a widespread resistance to the idea that this age group can live without coercion. In practice, *Taking Children Seriously* begins at many ages, depending on the growth of individual families. For those, however, who are fortunate to discover it before they become parents or very early on in their children's lives, there is no reason why consent-based living needs to be withheld from babies and toddlers.

The needs of young babies may be intense, but, in general, they are fairly simple in range. Food, warmth and physical closeness tend to feature high on the list. Despite the lack of verbal articulacy, most parents quickly become adept at interpreting the signals of what is liked and disliked. This is what TCS means when it credits babies with rationality. The theory is not that babies are born arguing the validity, (or not), of Hegel's dialectic, but rather that they are born with the ability constantly to create new knowledge and follow their intrinsic self-motivation and self-interest. As such, babies are rational and we can find common preferences with them. The same is true as babies grow into toddlers. We may only be able to use very simple words or we may need to rely on visual or practical demonstration, but we can definitely discern toddlers' preferences, and clearly see that toddlers are able to move to new preferences or, (in their own way), suggest new solutions to adults. Rationality does not require that children first reach a golden age of reason. It simply relies on not interfering with children's ability to express preferences and not preventing them from reaching new and mutual preferences.

Let us take Joe, a nine-month-old who comes across a bottle of bleach and starts trying to unscrew the lid. The laissez-faire neglectful solution is to leave him to it. He will soon learn not to mess with bleach! The coercive strategy is to take the bleach away from Joe, probably with a firm 'no', perhaps with an attempt at distraction if Joe is in a liberal household. The common-sense rationale is that the bleach could do Joe harm and that coercion is a lesser harm, (if it harms at all), than the risks of swallowing bleach. For Joe, something else is happening. His needs and desires are not being taken seriously. He begins to learn that, whilst his parents say they love him, they will still do mean things to him, (by his lights). Already, Joe is being given mixed messages about the correlation of love and hurt.

TCS suggests not that we glibly let our children fend for themselves, but that we work with the child to find something the child would prefer to play with or drink or shake or smell. It might be that Joe is simply after a drink. It might be that Joe would like a bottle of some harmless liquid that he can screw, unscrew, pour and sniff. It might be that this particular bottle is attractive and feels good to hold. Could the bleach be emptied into another container, the bottle scoured and another liquid put in to retain the feel? It might be that Joe would prefer an ice cream or a trip to the park or a big bowl of finger-paint mixture to anything that the bottle could offer. The point is that it is highly unlikely that nine-month-old Joe was trying to commit suicide with the bleach. It is possible for an adult on his side to work with him to find what he wanted to get out of the exploration, and to enable him to achieve it or move on to another better exploration.

Safety first

From sharp tools to fires to staying out alone, there are assumptions about externally imposed safety rules shared by conventional parenting and education. I want to argue that these actually compromise safety by impeding the growth of intrinsically motivated decisions about personal safety. Moreover, the rules impede the growth of knowledge, obscuring possible learning around with artificial boundaries.

Imagine two seven-year-old friends, Sadie and Lucy. They have just made an outdoor den in a field at the back of Lucy's house. They decide that they will have a feast in their new hide-away and Sadie runs home to collect some crisps and sweets. Lucy returns without any food as her Mum has told her that she does not want her to spoil her appetite for tea. Disappointed, Lucy suggests that they can pick some food of their own and turns her attention to some nearby berries. Sadie says they should ask an adult what they are. She says that she knows that some berries are delicious and good and others are harmful, even deadly. Lucy replies that this is silly. She insists that berries are just fruit and adds that if she asks her Mum she will just be shouted at and maybe smacked, because she is not allowed to eat anything that her Mum considers dirty and is not supposed to eat between meals. Sadie tries again to convince Lucy that they could ask Sadie's Mum, who has told her that some berries can hurt you even if you only take a little bit and that smaller bodies can get more hurt. She says that her mum has told her that some berries are not so strong and might just give you tummy ache or not do anything bad if you tried a bit. She points out that she and Lucy do not know what sort these are, so they really should ask someone to help them. Lucy says angrily that adults do not help children, they just tell them what to do. She adds that she knows her mum will just punish her for breaking the rules and she wants to find out for herself. Sadie replies that her mum does help her and she does not want to eat any berries without knowing more about them.

In this scenario it is the child who has been brought up with rules who is much more in danger. Lucy's information is much sketchier than Sadie's, because her rule-bound parents have seen no need to provide her with the truth that wild berries vary in strength and effect. They have replaced information with the simplistic rule of 'don't touch'. Lucy's desire to engage in illicit behaviour is also increased by the rule-bound mentality. She sees her parents as the opposition, to be thwarted, and hopes to be able to get away with doing something without their knowledge. This attitude makes no sense to Sadie, who, living in a TCS home, sees her parents as trusted advisors who will only say 'well, a few of these could make you feel quite ill and a lot could kill you' if that is really the truth. Sadie knows that if she were at home, not only would her parents offer good information about these particular berries, but would also help the girls find safe hedgerow foods to pick so that they could enjoy their feast. Sadie knows that her parents would help her to make her own good decision and would not treat her as though she was an irrational or suicidal imbecile. Lucy knows no such thing and the chance of being able to indulge in the forbidden over-rides her rationality and her friend's refutations.

The conventional parent might object that the solution is for Lucy's parents to become more coercive. After all, they could have insisted that Lucy plays only in their own garden. This is true, and whilst it may be a good idea for parents to discuss safe places to play, life can never be made totally risk free. Having a child who will seek advice before making informed decisions is a much safer option.

The conventional parent might insist that another thing that is extremely safe is to ensure that you have a child who just will not break the rules. They might argue that Lucy's parents had obviously not been strict enough and the rule had not been sufficiently impressed upon her. This is a dangerous argument. Some children, sadly, have wills that break easily; their creativity and drive to find their own solutions are soon crushed with even small amounts of coercion. Many children, however, are more resilient, and the force needed to impose mechanical rules can quickly spiral, making the home a virtual war zone.

Two-year old James, for example, has been told not to touch the electric sockets. His parents begin by saying 'no' and trying to distract him each time he approaches a socket. James continues to be interested, so the parents say 'no' more sternly and remove James to his bedroom for a few minutes each time he approaches a socket. James is undeterred, so his parents add a light slap to James' hand on each occasion, but still to no avail. Now James' parents reluctantly, but for his own good, decide to spank him each time he tries to touch a socket. James is very distressed by this development, but does not give up. Where can these conventional parents go next? Life in this household has become a long round of conflict. The electric sockets will be just one of many battles being fought.

The TCS parents will first examine their theories about electric sockets. Are they a danger to James? In most homes with modern wiring, the insulation is such that a child poking in a finger will come to absolutely no harm. If the socket is a real danger, perhaps this is the problem that the parents should really be addressing. In the meantime, they need to find ways to communicate the danger to James, ways to find a common preference around his safety that does not rely on lies or artificial rules that just beg to be broken.

Even if we succeed in making our children live by extrinsic rules, even if we can make them accept rules without having to resort to beatings, even if we choose our rules carefully and only impose a few rules that will tend to hold in most cases; even then, our children will not be as safe as children who are given honest information about risks - children who know that they can get all the help they need in negotiating risks, and are accustomed to finding the best solution for any particular situation.

We cannot foresee every situation. Life is risky, and there will always be tragedies whatever way we parent. The children most likely to be safe are those who can think most rationally, who can access advice without fear of coercion or lies, and who have no motivation to do something just because it is forbidden. TCS children will certainly take risks, but they will take them rationally, advisedly, and with the best preparation, to get the learning they want without exposure to unnecessary and unwanted danger. Ultimately, the only safety that any individual has is that which comes from intrinsic motivation. Assisting our children in developing this safety does them an enormous service. Coercing them to accept extrinsic safety rules leaves them exposed and vulnerable to irrational decisions. Moreover, such coercion impedes the growth of knowledge.

Five-year-old Darren loves to play with fire, but how he learns about it will depend on what kind of home he grows up in. Let us imagine Darren in a conventional household. The rule is that Darren must not play with fire. Fire is dangerous. He could hurt himself or even burn down the whole house and kill the whole family. Two things could happen. The first is that Darren will find a way secretly to break the rule. In this case, he will either satisfy himself that his parents are talking lies and nonsense and are not to be trusted, or he will have an accident of some nature, perhaps minor, perhaps more serious, but certainly avoidable if someone had helped him. The second is that Darren will obey the rule and cease all exploration in this area. In the short term, this may look fine to the casual observer, but Darren is left with irrational and untrue theories about fire that he will eventually pass on, and his own growth of knowledge in this area will have been cut off. Darren cannot learn about fire and combustibility and the properties of materials and all the lines of inquiry that might arise from such experimentation. In a laissez-faire household, by contrast, Darren could pursue his experimentation and learning, but would be more likely to do so dangerously, not having access to good advice and assistance.

Darren's life would be completely different in a TCS household. His parents would give him good safety information about fire, outlining the possible dangers, but without exaggeration or pressure. They would explore the kinds of experiments Darren would like to do and discuss the best ways to go about them. They would assess together which experiments he could do alone, which would require help, what safety devices would be good to have on hand and where the best place would be to conduct the experiments. Darren could develop good theories about fire, pursue his own intrinsic learning and stay safe.

Life and risks are intrinsically bound together. Sometimes we choose risks quite rationally in order to learn something or enjoy some particular experience. This said, there are many dangers that are avoidable. The safest course is to parent our children so that they will trust our advice, critically assess our best theories and make their own rational decisions.

Bodily autonomy

Diet, exercise, personal hygiene, health and sleep are all areas that present themselves to conventional parents as areas where control is needed. These are areas in which we constantly revise and develop our theories; yet, all too often, we expect our children to develop good theories whilst being coerced. There are two issues here for TCS parents to consider. The first is whether, as parents, we have any right at all to so much as pass comment on such personal matters. The second is whether our actual theories, if we do have a right or responsibility to share them, are correct.

Do we have the right to pass comment on what are essentially matters of bodily autonomy? If we were asked that question in relation to another adult, the likely answer would be 'no'. We recognise that people have the right to eat what they like, bathe when they like, keep fit in their own way (or not) and sleep when it suits them. Even if we are able to see that children deserve the same rights to bodily autonomy as adults, however, we might object that when we are living in close proximity with others, we do not expect them to assert their rights all the time. We might, for example, feel that it is not unreasonable to expect a certain level of personal hygiene from a husband or wife, or we might reasonably request a partner to wear a particular style of clothing for an important company dinner party. In the same way, we share space with our children. Although we have no *right* as such to dictate what they eat, when they shower, whether they should use deodorant and how much sleep they need, it can be quite reasonable to share our theories about these areas and to seek common preferences. This does not mean that children should automatically accept their parents' theories. It is simply a recognition that in close relationships there is an arena for comment and sharing, provided it does not become coercive hectoring and provided that the parent is willing to desist if no common preference is found.

Mandy is a teenager who is experimenting with her looks and dress. Some of her choices seem rather daring to her parents, but they are keen to respect her autonomy. Mandy is also interested in religious beliefs and practices. She tells her parents that she wants to spend some time visiting different places of worship, finding out more about different beliefs and what they might mean for her. Her parents advise her that her favourite short red skirt is likely to be seen negatively at both the local Church and the Mosque a few streets away. They tell her that she may not be taken seriously, and may even meet hostility. They suggest that more conventional clothing might help if she wants to be able to talk to people without eliciting negative judgements. Mandy decides that this is good advice and follows it.

A few weeks later her father tells her that some distant relatives are coming to stay. He says that they are rather conventional people who expect to be deferred to by young people. He asks that Mandy wear 'sensible' clothes while they are staying. Mandy thinks about this and decides that it is a bad idea. She tells her father that, in her own home, she feels that it is an unacceptable intrusion to dress according to the prejudices of virtual strangers whom she may very well never see again. She lets her father know that, while she was willing to make changes in order to visit other people in their own place of worship and to enable her to learn the most from her visits, she cannot see that this is a similar situation. She sympathises with the fact that her father will probably get adverse comments from these relatives, but she thinks that he is quite able to deal with this in his own home with people with whom he has no regular contact. After some thought, her father agrees that Mandy is right. He can probably deflect any criticism with gentle humour and need not be so anxious about the visit.

While we do not have a right to tell our children what to eat or wear, it is reasonable for us to make suggestions and share opinions, though we always need to remember that our theories might be wrong. When it comes to issues of bodily autonomy, food and sleep are the two areas that seem recurrently to cause the most concern. Food is an emotive area about which all sorts of claims and speculations abound. What is considered 'good for us' changes frequently on either scientific or quasi-scientific grounds. Even worse, there is a whole industry of dubious theories purporting to tell us that we should only eat what Stone Age people ate, or should follow recommended lists according to our blood group, or should eat only gluten on days of the week with a 'w' in them. In such a fast changing and confused arena, parents often aim to control what their children eat in the name of 'best interest'. Children are autonomous human beings, capable of making good decisions when given good information. We should certainly share our theories about food and nutrition and dental decay with our children, but we should not exaggerate, lie or claim to have found the final truth. Given our own fallibility and the shifting ground of this area of human knowledge, the likelihood of having the truth is very remote and our children may have very good criticisms to offer us.

The fear is that given free choice, children will gorge on an endless diet of cola, crisps and chocolate - but why should this happen? Certainly, children's intake of these items may rise from its former controlled or forbidden levels, especially when restraints are first lifted; but why should we assume that our children are so irrational that they will not be able to find a particular way of eating that works for them? We are not simply leaving them to it, after all, but are there with advice and suggestions. A child is just as likely to make objectively good decisions as an adult. What is more, even when adults feel that children are making bad decisions, they cannot be sure that this is the case. If the parents are offering theories that are convincing on their own merits, there is every chance that the child will agree. Parents should be wary of damaging their children's mental well-being and sense of autonomy for the sake of a dietary theory that might be out of vogue in two years' time.

Letting go of the control of our children's sleep patterns can be another major hurdle in finding win-win solutions. Henry is a three-year-old who likes to be awake at night. His parents see this as a problem, but can gradually come to see that it is possible to find a common preference with Henry. They might decide to take turns to stay awake with Henry. They might decide that the parent with a job to get up for early each morning should get some sleep and the other parent adapts his or her sleeping pattern to Henry's pattern. This parent might discover that the night-time is a great time to be awake. She might enjoy 24 hour shopping with Henry or find the quiet is conducive to writing the novel she always wanted to produce, while Henry watches favourite videos or plays nearby, knowing that his parent is available if he needs anything. They might find that Henry would gladly sleep earlier in the evening if some condition were changed, perhaps the lighting or noise levels or temperature or having someone with him while he is falling asleep. They might find that they can both sleep while Henry stays awake playing if he can play quietly in their bedroom or close by or watch a video in their room as they are falling asleep. They might find that the problem is not that Henry likes to be awake into the night, which they can accommodate with some creative thinking. Rather, the problem is that Henry is booked into day-care at 8.30 a.m. each morning and the late nights mean that he would prefer to sleep till about 9a.m. or sometimes later. Can the family take Henry along to day-care later? Can one or both of the parents alter working schedules? Does Henry want to be in day-care at all? If not, how is the family going to solve that problem?

By working creatively on a given set of evolving problems, common preferences can be found. Starting with set ideas about what time children of three should be in bed or how many hours sleep a three year old *must* have will not produce solutions, only battles which someone must lose. Individuals vary. Some of us need or would prefer ten-hour blocks of sleep. Some of us thrive on very little sleep or prefer several shorter periods of sleep. Some of us relish mornings and others the night. Why should children be denied the right to find the pattern that works for their particular body and mind at a particular stage of their life?

A common objection is that people have to learn to fit into 'the real world'. In fact, the real world, which we all live in, is becoming ever more flexible. School is not compulsory. Most appointments can be arranged at our convenience. Work patterns are increasingly complex and open to negotiation. Leisure, shopping and so much else is increasingly available 'out of hours' in supermarkets and high streets, as well as via the Internet and new technologies. Event-driven living is replacing the agrarian concept of rising and sleeping with the sun or the industrial concept of nine till five or shift workdays. Children who are able to grow up respecting their own preferences, and without the sleep disturbances so common to those of us who have grown up with coercion, will be best placed to take part in a flexible world with a sense of making their own choices.

Ultimately, we cannot control our children's bodies, nor should we. Children who are repeatedly coerced around food are highly likely to become adults with food problems, possibly even serious eating disorders. Children who are forced to sleep or wake at times that do not work for them are likely to be tomorrow's insomniacs. Children whose bodily autonomy is not respected can hardly be blamed for having little self-respect or for taking dangerous and avoidable risks in attempts to gain some self-control, whether through anorexia, taking drugs without information or becoming irrationally averse to taking any exercise.

As with safety, the best way to help our children make good decisions about nutrition, exercise, sleep, hygiene, hair length or any other issue of bodily autonomy, is not through coercion, but through rational conjecture and refutation. In the privileged and responsible role of parents we can be trusted advisors in these areas, but common preferences are much easier to find when we respect and truly believe that our children are autonomous human beings in their own right.

Pulling together

Conventional parenting theory strongly suggests that children have to learn to lose, often a great deal of the time. Building win-win situations often appears elusive, even impossible, to parents who are used to such conventional thinking, but win-win solutions are possible, always in theory and, as we become accustomed to finding common preferences, increasingly in practice. Many conflicts seem to reach an impasse simply because we are so ready to set the supposed good of the family group against the preferences of the individual. We do well to remember that the good of the family group is not being served if in fact one of its members is suffering. The group's good only becomes a possibility when everyone within it prefers what is happening.

This myth usually presumes that whatever the parents deem to be important at any given moment is definitive of the family good. If the parents think it is teatime and everyone should sit down together and eat the same food, then this is characterised as the family good. Often, tidying up, chores and sibling rivalry are areas in which this conventional wisdom operates most strongly.

Fifteen-year-old Amy lives with her mum (a sculptor), her dad (a therapist), ten-year-old brother Adam and sister Jess (aged six). Her parents are trying to be non-coercive, but they have an entrenched theory that the family has a form of contract to one another and should each do their share as regards chores. Jess quickly learned to take advantage of her status as youngest to avoid coercion, but Adam and Amy seem to be in constant conflict about chores. Sometimes they will spontaneously join in with polishing or vacuuming, but they resent being pulled away from watching TV or doing something they enjoy to do particular tasks at particular times. The parents see this resentment as intransigence and irrationality, but Amy has some counter arguments. She points out that her mother's attic studio is always messy, so surely her mother can see that tidiness is not essential always and everywhere; rather it is a matter of such things as function, taste and individual comfort level. Amy points out that the reason for having a pristine hallway and stairs is that her father's clients come through that way to reach his therapy room. Not all children live in homes with this kind of dual use, and it is not her responsibility to provide a work environment for her father. She argues that she did not consent to being born and does not feel that she has actually had a choice about entering into any contract with her parents. Amy says that she is quite happy with a certain level of mess. It is her mother and father who have the highest standards and comfort requirements, so they should find ways of getting their needs met that do not involve coercing her and Adam. Amy also points out that the reason that they cannot ever find a solution, instead, going round and round in circles and unhappy compromises, is that they do not even have the same problem. Her parents' problem is how to keep the house clean. Since they have a theory about a necessary level of tidiness, they constantly look for any mess and focus on this. Amy's (and Adam's) problem is that they feel very unhappy when their parents clearly disapprove of them, but also feel unhappy when they are doing things against their will. The children have theories that parental approval and being able to do the things they want are important components in their lives and they are constantly looking for ways to maximise these. Unfortunately, the tidying the house saga compromises both areas. Amy suggests that she would be happy to help her parents solve their problem and asks that they help her with her problem, too.

Having identified the problems, Amy and her parents finally set about looking for solutions. Lots of suggestions are made. They could hire someone to come in and clean the house. Amy's father says he does not like the idea of a stranger in his therapy room where he keeps confidential records. Amy suggests a locked cabinet. Adam says he does not think there are enough bins and laundry baskets in the house. Jess adds that her friends have a lot more machines in their kitchen, like a dishwasher and microwave. Mum says that she is constantly uneasy with strangers coming and going in the house and feels under pressure to please these strangers. She suggests that they dig out the plans they had for an extension to the side of the house so that the therapy practice would not intrude on their home and she would not feel so anxious about tidiness. This would also give space for Amy and Jess to have their own rooms, which would solve other problems. Everyone talks about the household chores that they enjoy even occasionally. They agree that those things that no one likes or which no one would enjoy regularly should be the things they pay for help with.

If everyone were happy, the discussion might end there, with recognition that no one within the family should be put in a position where they feel either coerced or disapproved of. A new problem, however, might be thrown up by the solutions that have been offered. Adam might ask how much these solutions are going to cost and wonder whether paying for all this will mean putting off the purchase of a computer he has been longing for. This might lead to prioritising the solutions or refining them or even to going back to the original problem and criticising the theory that the house ever needs to be as tidy as the parents first suggested. They will keep going until they have a genuine common preference because it is spurious to assert that the good of the group sometimes has to take precedence over the good and happiness of any one. The group is made up of the family members. If one of them is unhappy, then the good of the group is not being served, no matter how much it is pretended otherwise.

Manners and mores

Adults often expect and require a degree of respect from children that they do not feel the need to reciprocate. Many children are taught never to tell lies, whilst their parents routinely lie to them. 'We cannot afford that chocolate bar'; 'You'll become ill if you watch too much television'; 'All your teeth will drop out if you don't brush them twice a day' and so on, are simply examples of a huge repertoire of stock responses that many parents use for convenience or control. In the film *Liar, Liar* the father (Jim Carrey) explains to his son Max (Justin Cooper) that adults have to tell lies in order to get by in the world or to remain polite. Carrey explains that without 'white' lies, life would be untenable. In the scenes that follow, we see how difficult life can become when his character, a divorce lawyer, is compelled to be bluntly honest because of Max's birthday wish that his father cannot lie. Adults can plainly see that lying is not always a bad thing and is sometimes a very good thing; for example, few people would think that being truthful about the whereabouts of a Jewish family, if asked by a Nazi soldier, would be moral. Yet, despite this, we are much more simplistic in our expectations of children's honesty. Children who use lies for their own survival are easily labelled as sneaky and untrustworthy when they may in fact be acting in their own best interest or lying for some other moral reason.

Another required feature of children's 'manners' is that they should not interrupt adults. In adult conversations, there is a constant to and fro of interruption that is taken as part of normal banter and is acceptable in most circumstances; (exceptions might be when men dominate conversations to the exclusion of female colleagues or when interruptions become aggressive). When children are doing the interrupting, however, there are often accusations of rudeness and disrespect. What is actually occurring is the mobilisation of a pecking order. Children are at the bottom of a hierarchy. What they have to say is deemed to be of less value. If they intrude on an adult conversation, it must be for some reason that is trivial and easily dismissed. 'Go and play and don't bother me unless someone breaks a leg or there is blood,' may be said in joking tones, but it reveals an attitude that children's concerns are intrinsically less worthy of attention than anything an adult could be saying. There may be times when an adult needs some privacy or a set period of time to achieve a task, and there is no reason why common preferences cannot be found to ensure such times. There may equally be times when children want uninterrupted private time. That said, there is no room in consensual relationships for simply presuming that there is a hierarchy in which children's concerns, needs and comments are discounted and ranked last. The appearance of conventional 'good' manners is not as important as taking our children seriously.

Children who always say 'please' and 'thank you' and who speak with deference towards adults complement the conventional dream of truthful, unobtrusive children. There is no intrinsic reason why children accustomed to being taken seriously and who live in households where consent is fundamental should be rude and aggressive, but neither is there any reason for such children to be artificially grateful or pleading. Such children are likely to be used to speaking as human persons of equal worth. There are times when a 'please' or 'thank you' is simply a small token of courtesy that might be used by adults and children alike without any coercive undertones. If it is required that a child say please for everything he receives, from food to toys, from trips to attention, however, then something is wrong. Should slaves be grateful for emancipation? Should women be grateful for the vote and equal pay? Those groups might certainly appreciate these things in their lives and might admire those who helped them gain these rights, but they are basic human rights. Is a child any less human, even to the extent that he should be grateful if his parent feeds him or spends thirty seconds listening to him? Parents have a duty towards their children. Gratitude is not owed and cannot ultimately be compelled, even if children are forced to mouth it. That is not to say that relationships in which people feel thankful for one another cannot or should not develop, but such feelings are not to be coercively manufactured.

A question of resources

Learning to win and getting what we want are not the same as a child having everything at the snap of his fingers, but neither should parents assume that there are resources over which they have no control to help their children. This is particularly the case with budget constraints or limited time. We do not have to be rich to take our children seriously, but we do have to be creative. Learning to win is a matter of creatively finding common preferences. This will certainly lead to very new ways of considering and using family budgets, but it does not lead to inevitable bankruptcy. Moreover, things actually acquired may look very different from any initial wish list.

Many times, conventional parents tell children that they cannot afford a particular wanted item when the truth is that it is simply not their priority. If children are to be taken seriously, there must be some basic honesty and openness about family finances. Is more being spent on fuel than necessary simply because parents have not researched alternative suppliers? Does the 'essential' food bill include regular adult 'take-aways' when the children are told that take-away pizzas are an unaffordable extravagance? Do the children agree that expensive furniture and new clothes are vital, whilst extra televisions for family members are out of reach? Would the children rather use the money from piano classes for a year on a trip to Disney land or vice versa? The questions and answers will be endlessly various between different families. The point is simply that everything can be questioned. Sometimes the answers will be as surprising as they are creative.

Twelve-year-old twins, Toby and Daisy, would like to have more technology available. There is often too much competition for the family's one television and, under the previous coercive family regime, they were often expected to give way to their little brother, Jim (aged six). Toby would like more opportunities to explore the Internet and design web sites, but the one family computer is over-subscribed and his father's work seems to take precedence. Toby has watched the Discovery channel at a friend's house and would particularly like a television with a cable connection. Daisy loves movies and would like a video to go with a television in her own room. Jim adds that he would like to have the cable cartoon channel and a Playstation. The family sits down and talks about the wish list, at which point Mum adds that she would like the film channel and Dad says he would like a more modern computer with specifications more suited to his current work. The family is not rich and the wish list involves money. Dad suggests he could take on an extra freelance contract for a limited time or Mum could do some agency nursing (her former career). Jim says he does not like it when Mum is not there at bedtime. Toby points out that he was hoping for some time soon with Dad to help him with some programming. Daisy says she would be happy to contribute some recent birthday money from grandparents and Toby agrees that he would like to do this, too. Toby suggests that they could clear the attic and do a boot-sale and could probably raise at least another £100 that way and have some fun doing it. This prompts Dad to remember that he has been meaning to sell an old record collection for some time. Mum says that she and Dad had been discussing the two living room sofas. Both are rather worn and shabby and she had suggested taking out a loan to buy new ones. She now thinks that perhaps the sofas could hold up for another year or two and instead they could use a loan for a second computer. Toby suggests that some of the other items could be obtained second hand or reconditioned. Daisy suggests they make a priority list and that they should talk about how each of them might feel about allowing other family members to use items in their own rooms. Whether the family end up with all of the proposed items - or none of them, or something completely different - is not the issue. There is no fixed outcome, except that it should be mutually agreed. Whether the family budget is enormous or extremely modest, the key is creativity and not deciding beforehand that something *must* be done in a certain way or that something else is simply not worth considering.

Being creative with time is as important as being creative with money. All too often, adults set up time constraints without sufficiently thinking through the implications for children or considering alternatives that might be required. Most families need at least one adult to work for a family income. Most families will, at some point, need to make appointments with doctors, lawyers, plumbers. Many families will schedule classes or driving lessons or plane flights. It is not that these things do not matter, but that they do not matter more than our children. They are areas in which we can reach common preferences. Can we rearrange work commitments, either in terms of time or venue, to fit in better with family preference? Can we build in flexibility with certain kinds of appointments? Can we arrange alternative care or activities for our children so that they are not committed to unnecessary journeys on our behalf?

Pam has an early morning doctor's appointment. She has made the appointment at a difficult time in that her five-year-old daughter, Ellen, likes to wake up slowly and enjoy a leisurely breakfast while watching a favourite cartoon. Pam's husband Steve can often start work at a flexible time, but has an important client to meet. The doctor Pam prefers to see works part-time and her appointments tend to get booked up well in advance. Pam is very concerned about a particular health issue and does not feel that it would be a good idea to wait much longer. The conventional answer would be to take Ellen along, whatever her protests, and to argue that her distress is nothing in comparison to her mother's current anxiety and needs. Some parents would even claim that if Ellen objects, it is she who is being coercive and not Pam. Coercion requires power. Children do not have power over their parents, whereas parents have an automatic power that is easily abused and widely supported. This one instance of coercion may do no damage to Ellen, but we cannot know that. It is immoral to take such a risk and highly disrespectful of Ellen's autonomy.

So what can Pam do? She could ask the elderly lady over the road, who loves spending time with Ellen, to come in and stay with her for an hour. She could explain to Steve that this appointment is very important to her, so important that it might be worth his considering changing his appointment with clients. She could reconsider whether one of the other practice doctors who are more available might not be just as sympathetic and helpful, and rearrange to mid-day when Ellen is happy to come along, or to evening when Steve is back home. She could talk to Ellen about making the trip to the doctor's a special and fun event. Perhaps Ellen could sleep in a comfy tracksuit the night before and be tucked into the car with a blanket and warm drink for the journey. They could take a favourite snack to the waiting room and a favourite picture book, or borrow Steve's hand-held Gameboy or his portable cassette player with headphones and story tapes. They could go out for a special breakfast after the appointment or have a breakfast of popcorn at the nearby cinema while seeing a cartoon movie that Ellen has expressed interest in.

When we begin from a fixed point and fixed preferences, we are unlikely to succeed in living consensually. Instead, we will end up with coercion or self-sacrifice. When we are willing to let go of the myth of inevitable and immutable outcomes, we free up the creativity to find common preferences. It might be that the solution will contain one or more of the initial starting points. Pam might keep her appointment without any coercion, for example. The point is simply that real common preferences are found when no one is insisting that there can be only one possible outcome.

Necessary knowledge

Education is a crucial parenting issue for conventional and TCS parents alike. The supposed need to 'know' certain things or the drive to learn certain things solely in order to keep options open for the future are cornerstones of conventional educational and parenting theory, but are inimical to taking children seriously.

We cannot predict the future for our children. By helping them to live their lives now and learn what they want to know now, we can ensure that the knowledge they have is optimum for the particular individual. We help our children know that new knowledge can always be gained. The push to instil a body of necessary knowledge into our children arises largely from misunderstanding and fear. If we do not make our children learn to read or recite their multiplication tables, will we be doing them a terrible disservice by setting them up for only dead end jobs and a life without choices? If we do not force our children to listen to music or read the plays of Shakespeare, will they forever miss out on rich cultural and aesthetic experiences? If we do not impose some basic requirements on our children's learning, will they simply learn nothing?

Children who are coerced by neglect risk enforced ignorance and the closing down of their abilities and passion. This is not the case for children whose autonomy is being respected within homes where parents are providing resources, stimulation, suggestions and support in response to the intrinsic learning motivation of their children. Children will learn to read, multiply or take photographs when they have an intrinsic need to acquire that particular skill. Children who are adept at creative problem solving and in finding ways to fulfil their preferences in the present are not likely to stop doing so simply because they reach the age of sixteen or eighteen. Children with choices will become adults with choices. If we do not impose agendas on our children's learning, but instead help them to learn what they want to learn, how could they possibly learn 'nothing'?

Wasting time

Alongside the mythology of an essential body of knowledge that must be taught at all costs, there is often the idea that learning can only be taking place when certain so-called educational activities are taking place. Other activities - often activities which children particularly enjoy - are conventionally deemed to be of less value or even harmful. Playing computer games, watching so called 'non-

educational' TV shows and videos or climbing trees are all things
that can be denigrated as wasting time. The TCS philosophy offers
a radically different perspective on such 'time wasting'. Time is
wasted when it is being spent on things that are extrinsically
motivated; that is, when children are doing things they have to do
rather than things they want to do. It is possible that our children
will make some bad choices, which, by their own lights, turn out to
be mistakes. Mistakes can be learnt from, especially when they are
our own mistakes and not someone else's imposed agenda. Life is
full of risk and uncertainty. It might be that a childhood spent
playing with Lego and climbing trees will not lead to a career in
medicine, but it is highly probable that a childhood spent learning
Shakespeare and physics at someone else's insistence will lead to a
life of chronic self-sacrifice and constantly living for tomorrow
while today is miserable. It certainly seems feasible that a childhood
spent creatively solving the problem of how to get the most out of
life right now will be far from wasted, whatever the particular
activities happen to be.

The value of suffering

Does all of this emphasis on winning simply give children a false
notion of what the world is like? Conventional parenting theories
insist that we need to experience a certain level of frustration,
hardship and suffering in order to survive in the real world. It must
always be remembered that we all live in the real world. Our
circumstance may differ dramatically, but there is still only one
world in which we can live. Living well in it is not 'unreal'. Parents
who want to impose some frustration or suffering on their child's
experience are generally motivated to do so not out of cruelty, but
out of fear that otherwise their children will not be prepared for
whatever life holds. We have, however, already seen that acting for
someone else's assumed 'own good' is not a good reason for doing
anything. We could be wrong. We do not, in any case, have the
right to so fundamentally compromise another's autonomy. The
argument for deliberately frustrating our children or sometimes
purposefully setting out to 'show' them that they cannot always
'have their own way' is very similar to the argument for natural
consequences and is similarly flawed. When parents frustrate their
children, they are choosing to do so. The hurt is not inevitable, but
imposed and artificial. Life contains enough risks and enough
learning opportunities for children to see for themselves that bad
things happen. They can learn how to tackle and handle the real
tragedies and complex problems by having lots of access to

information and good models of how to problem-solve creatively. We do not prepare for a journey to a famine-stricken country by starving ourselves, but by building up our strength and learning all we can about basic nutrition and survival. There is no intrinsic value in being in a state of distress. It only serves to crush our ability to think rationally.

Learning to win

We live in a society where children are routinely deprived of the common rights of humanity, where they often cannot choose what to eat or wear, whom they associate with, when they can sleep, what they can learn or even what they can enjoy as leisure. Love is neither compensation nor justification for such a total lack of autonomy. The suffering that arises is not character building or a preparation for living in the real world, but rather, damages the ability to problem solve creatively and consider solutions rationally. It perpetuates an acceptance of suffering and an inability to follow one's preferences into adulthood. Children whose autonomy is respected do not expect never to have to solve problems or that life will be handed to them on a plate or that they will never have to work hard at realising their preferences. Autonomous children know that problem solving is a feature of real life and growth, that risk is inevitable and that change and criticism and new solutions are always going to be needed. What they do not do is conflate problems with suffering or effort with sacrifice. When we live in an ethos of consent, creativity and rationality, artificial boundaries become irrelevant and are replaced instead by a life in which learning and winning are fundamental.

- Reason does not develop with age: we are born with reason and we use it best when we are accustomed to a lifetime of being taken seriously.
- Rationality, creativity, being able to trust advice and having access to information, are more likely to promote safety than following artificial rules.
- We might offer advice and opinions about personal issues, but parents should be highly respectful of their children's bodily autonomy.
- If one person is unhappy with or distressed by a solution, then it is spurious to assert that this is for the good of the family. The good of the family is served only when all its members are winning.
- Our children are unique, autonomous and more important than conventions on manners and appearance.

- You do not have to have untold riches or twenty-six hours in the day, but you do have to be creative.
- Your child will not be prevented from choosing a career in astrophysics because you neglected to force him to study maths at the age of twelve, but he could be chronically disabled from following all kinds of paths if he is not assisted creatively and rationally to solve his current problems now, however trivial they might appear.
- Learning is sabotaged and time is wasted when children are doing extrinsically mandated activities, not when they are pursuing their own interests, however uneducational these might look to the casual observer or anxious parent.
- Suffering for its own sake has no value. Life contains enough real problems, risks and challenges without manufacturing hardships.

Chapter eight

Your worst nightmare

A life of learning by winning might seem conceivable in certain areas, but most of us have deeply ingrained reservations and entrenched theories about wholesale autonomy. A range of adult fears commonly arises when we consider removing coercion from our children's lives. There is a common fear that if given such autonomy, children will become anti-social, a fear that disregards the role of coercion in contributing to anti-social, self-destructive and self-defeating behaviours.

Coercion and the anti-social child

Fear and control are common partners. Many parents are afraid that if they are not the ones controlling the child's behaviour, then that behaviour will be 'out of control' rather than within the child's control. Much of this fear arises from watching scenarios where parental control has disintegrated or where parents are so disengaged from their children that the children make increasingly bizarre bids to be noticed and taken seriously. Parents might point to children who are both anti-social and self-destructive and say 'Look, his parent didn't manage to control him, so we will have to try harder if we don't want our children to end up like that'. Others argue, 'Look, her parents took no interest and simply let her do anything she liked, no questions asked, and what a mess that's resulted in'. These are not arguments against taking children seriously, giving children autonomy or living consensually within our families.

The prisons are not full of TCS children. Whilst TCS is not primarily concerned with outcome-based parenting, I think we can confidently predict that, unless TCS children are living under unjust and illiberal laws, this situation is likely to continue. Self-destructive people who seem to be as much beyond their **own** powers of control as anyone else's are not rational, creative, undamaged individuals. They are those contorted by coercion damage, not those happily pursuing their own best interests.

Why should a child who believes that her parents are on her side, who knows that following her own interests will be supported and facilitated and who believes that solutions can always be found, need to become a sociopath? Many children who become as severely self-destructive as they are anti-social grow up in homes that veer wildly between strict parenting and neglectful parenting, homes where they can be beaten one moment, ignored the next and screamed at the next.

The argument that what we need is more control is false. We cannot possibly be there controlling everything our child does from birth to sixteen years old. We physically cannot live their lives. Our children are going to be making decisions and they are going to be making some of those decisions when we are not immediately available. Having built up a repertoire of conversations about every aspect of morality, having spent considerable time sharing criticisms with our children and helping them remain and become creative, rational problem solvers, we can expect that our children will make the best decisions by their own lights at that particular time. We can expect that some mistakes will be made, but making mistakes is an opportunity for learning, not a signal that our autonomy ought to be taken away from us. We can also expect that sometimes our children will not make the decisions that we would have made or advised. Taking children seriously is not an exercise in getting our children to do exactly what we would want by roundabout, manipulative means, even in our absence. Our children will be making new knowledge and pursuing their own interests. This will not always look like our prescriptions of best interests.

Even in the most rigidly controlling families, where punishment is an ever-present threat and behaviour is controlled by fear, control is ultimately an illusion. Being afraid is as much a motivation for ever more creative acts of deviousness as it is for doing what parents desire; meanwhile, the ability to think rationally about areas pressurised by such chronic coercion becomes an increasingly remote possibility.

The argument that children who are left to their own devices often come up with bad morality or behave in self-destructive ways indicates that children need less autonomy and more firm guidance, is equally flawed. Parents who are serious about living in consent-based relationships with their children do not neglect them. They constantly offer their theories of morality, criticism and information; they facilitate access to conflicting information and counter arguments; and they continually engage in conjecture and refutation with their children. What they do not do is cross the line of superseding their children's autonomy or act as if they are infallible. Children who are taken seriously are neither left to their own devices nor coerced.

The selfish monster

Even if we accept that the extremities of anti-social behaviour arise from hideous coercion either through abuse or neglect, we might still have reservations. So our children may not be likely to turn into bank robbers and mass murderers, but will they be pleasant people? Are they not more likely to be spoilt brats who grow up into selfish, petulant adults?

Such questions arise from a number of misunderstandings of self-interest. Firstly, why do we need to oppose self-interest and altruism? We are sadly used to the idea that if we are enjoying something, it must be at someone else's expense; whereas, if we are suffering, we are helping someone else. Is this really the case? As a parent, I can derive huge satisfaction and pleasure from helping my child get what he wants. It is something I prefer to do. I am at once pursuing my own and my child's interest. As a worker, I can derive enormous satisfaction from my job, or I can choose to do it to support the people I love or to benefit the community. These goals do not need to be mutually exclusive. I am doing what I prefer on one or many levels and others benefit. Similarly, a scientist can pursue her passion and make discoveries that are of enormous benefit to humanity, or a researcher can follow his passion and create new knowledge of enormous consequence to many lives. It is when we are following our intrinsic motivation that we are both at our most self-interested and most creative, and likely to benefit others in a multiplicity of ways.

Secondly, these questions wrongly assume that we can get inside the minds of others, particularly our children, and label their motivations. Why should a child who wants what he wants be called a 'brat'? What is it that makes us resent his clarity and self-knowledge and sense of self-worth? Are we threatened by attributes that we were not allowed to develop for ourselves as children? Are we afraid that it will mean that our own needs must be subverted? Do we worry that we will have to jump immediately to order and sacrifice our own autonomy? If we have allowed ourselves to enter a cycle of self-sacrifice, then we are not really taking our children any more seriously than we are taking ourselves seriously, and need to address that problem rather than blame our children for it. Having children who can clearly state their initial preferences is a bonus in the process of finding common preferences, not a threat to our own autonomy.

When children experience for themselves relationships of consent in which the needs of others can be taken seriously without infringing their own needs and wants, then they have no reason to fear the needs of others. When children experience the benefits of finding common preferences, then the needs and wants of others become part of the pool of creativity available to them, rather than threats to preferred solutions. A child who will not listen to anything other than his first preference and who irrationally clings to this even when there may be solutions he could enjoy much more. is a child who is used to losing and is determined to resist losing again. Being 'self-centred' or 'pleasing ourselves' does not have to stand in opposition to finding common preferences and benefiting others with our creativity. This is a false and pernicious dichotomy that taking our children seriously can overcome.

Losing control

Adults who have the capacity to determine their own lives and who have the rationality and creativity to live as autonomous people with enlightened self-interest do not routinely act in immoral, self-destructive or abusive ways. Yet, we often assume that given the same rights, respect and autonomy, children will do just that. Why? Children may make decisions that we think are bad for them or even wrong in general. Even if we are right, however, it is highly likely that these decisions will arise from the irrationality that accompanies coercion damage. We are not going to convince our children to become more rational and more creative and less self-destructive by coercing them some more. We do not get from a bad situation to a better one by increasing the condition that originally led to the bad situation. It should also be remembered that we might be wrong. It might well be that our child, even a previously coerced child, is in fact not making a bad or immoral decision. They might be making the best and most rational decision possible and one that we, with our own coercion damage and entrenched theories, cannot appreciate. Rational persuasion, conjecture and refutation, creative problem solving, sharing of theories without deciding the outcome for someone else, are all we can offer. The more we offer these, the more effective they become.

Winning without harm

TCS is a theory about how we learn. It is about problem-solving and the growth of knowledge and, as such, is very well placed to enable children to go on to a lifetime of creative problem-solving.

- Living a life of rational self-interest gives the flexible and creative tools for negotiating everyday problems and situations.

- Children getting what they want are not only engaged in genuine learning, but are also pursuing a moral approach to decisions.

- Acting out of self-interest is not monstrous or dangerous, but is a way of maximising best interest and creativity in general. When people follow their intrinsic motivation and self-interest, they maximise the very creativity that is vital to new ideas and progress for everyone.

- Individual happiness is a building block of progress, not an obstacle to it. The real world benefits most from creative, rational, self-interested, intrinsically motivated problem-solvers.

- Genuinely rational and creative self-interested people are constantly in pursuit of better knowledge, better theories, better solutions, new learning. This being so, they are not threatened by input or criticism, even when it contradicts a current piece of understanding.

- Children, like adults, make mistakes, but mistakes, as much as solutions, can provide points of growth.

- No system of parenting can predict the future for our children or guarantee them a life without problems. Such a life would, in any case, be sterile and empty of any growth of knowledge.

- By fostering their autonomy and building models of consent, flexibility, creativity and rationality, TCS gives children the freedom to find their own solutions in the real world and gives the world the prospect of highly creative thinkers from whom to benefit.

Chapter nine

Learning for all

Taking Children Seriously demands an enormous shift not only in how we think about children, but how we think about learning and life itself. Consent-based parenting, in which everyone wins, is the only lifestyle that does not damage autonomy and which allows for a consistently positive framework for negotiating family living and learning.

An environment for learning

Taking Children Seriously is not so much a parenting theory as a moral theory for family interaction and an educational theory about how knowledge grows. If we assume that coercion damages thinking, then a non-coercive environment must be the best learning environment possible. We do not think rationally about areas that we associate with distress. Distress lessens our grasp of rationality and creativity and, so, hampers our learning. That does not mean that all coerced people will grow up stupid and ignorant, but it does mean that in areas in which people experience coercion they are later likely to encounter greater numbers of thinking difficulties. It also means that areas of creativity are being nipped in the bud. So we might end up with, for example, a maths genius who cannot form intimate relationships and has very poor practical money handling skills, or an artist who finds every journey horrifically stressful and cannot think rationally about doing laundry, and so on.

This is not to say that TCS is an outcome-based parenting philosophy. The idea is not to produce the 'best' product, but to facilitate the child to live the best life by her own lights, which will not happen if we introduce thinking problems along the way through systematic coercion. Eradicating coercion then becomes fundamental to real education.

True learning is about gaining knowledge in those areas in which one wants to gain knowledge. It is quite possible to force our children to learn certain things in a behaviourist, outcome-based fashion. TCS, however, proposes that this is both morally wrong and will result in thinking damage in one or more areas. The key is intrinsic motivation, learning the things we want to learn. Who better to know what learning is most needed, wanted and appropriate, than the person himself? What other form of learning could be more efficient? Learning is something that takes place in an individual's mind - it cannot be poured in as though people were empty buckets waiting to be filled. Knowledge grows when it is intrinsic to the learner and only taking children seriously can give the degree of autonomy needed for this process to flourish.

Living consensually with our children impacts on every area of life. We cannot respect our children's autonomy if we are choosing what they should and should not learn. Although, in many, if not most cases, this will mean that children will choose home-based education as the optimum context for their autonomous learning, some children will choose school environments. When children are free to choose whether or not to be in school, they are free to take what they need or want from the experience. Their freedom transforms the nature of their relationship with the institution, and they know that their parents will assist them in dealing with the institution. Autonomy in education, as in life, is not about the style of learning, but about who has the control and motivation.

An inclusive paradigm

Living consensually with our children is a moral principle to be applied to all parent-child relationships. It is not just another parenting theory that might be applicable to only some children. TCS is not just for parents of especially bright children, or especially compliant children, or especially reasonable children. I have heard the objection that TCS is all very well if it 'works', or that it is fine if you have the 'right' sort of children on whom it will work. This objection totally misses the point of making the paradigm shift needed to live consensually within families. The question is not whether the theory 'works', but whether it is ever 'right' to coerce another autonomous human being, by virtue of their age or any other criteria.

Let us think of another area of morality to sharpen the question: is it right for husbands to beat their wives? Most people in this society at this time would say 'No! This type of coercion between a husband and wife is wrong.' Getting back to parents and children, the first question that parents contemplating TCS need to ask themselves is: Is coercion a proper way to treat my children? If the answer is no, then questions of whether it is practical or not become issues of finding ways to do the right thing, rather than ways of justifying why we have to do the wrong thing.

It is not moral to rob another human of his or her autonomy in order to produce the specimen that parents most desire. Many theories of parenting are primarily concerned with how little Sam is going to 'turn out'. There is a strong cultural pull towards proving that Sam is going to 'do well' or 'do us proud'. This is perhaps especially true if we are already going against the flow of convention by home educating and feel that we are under scrutiny to show that our way is just as good, if not better, by producing results. TCS assumes that every individual of any age is an autonomous agent. TCS assumes that it is wrong to coerce your own child. If this is the case, then trying to work towards specific outcomes in parenting, whether to seek cultural approval or for our own inner glow, is not supportable. Many of the parenting philosophies that do advocate outcomes do so in very reasonable language, and look as though they have very laudable goals, which any right-thinking person would support. What could be wrong with wanting your child to be happy, flexible, goal-orientated, and morally upright? The problem is simply that all such terms tend to be loaded with agenda and sliding meanings. TCS promotes the child's own autonomy by his or her own lights. The likelihood is that this will have good effects in the child's life, but the child must be in control of defining those effects. We must share our own morality with the child, but the child must ultimately be free to decide how to act. There is no testable end product. We are talking about autonomous human beings brought up in fallible human households, not control specimens who can become advertisements for how well we parented.

Taking Children Seriously proposes no blue-print solutions to problems. It is essentially a process rather than a set of guidelines, and a moral way of relating rather than just another outcome-based parenting theory. It is this that enables the theory to encompass anyone and everyone.

Living to learn

Childcare 'experts' sometimes propose that giving our children 'firm boundaries' is a way of giving them the security they need and crave. It is true that such artificial boundaries can give a sense of safety, but they often do so at a high cost. Along with the protection comes a hunger for a lifetime of security and certainty, an unwillingness to ask too many uncomfortable questions, and a dangerous willingness to obey without question. Fostering intrinsic security, however, is a much more complex process. To be able to find solutions; to enter into a process of conjecture and refutation; to listen to and weigh criticism and advice before making decisions; to take responsibility for one's decisions: this is another kind of security, which is eminently more valuable.

Taking Children Seriously proposes a process of finding common preferences by which each problem can find its unique solution. Working with this process demands a whole new paradigm that transforms life into a learning adventure unmatched by anything conventional parenting can offer.

CONVENTIONAL PARENTING	CONSENT-BASED PARENTING
The parent is authoritative. This may be a strict authority, or a liberal regime, in which the parent is the 'ultimate' or 'bottom line' arbitrator.	The parent acknowledges fallibility. The parent offers trusted advice, theories and criticism.
The conventional parent may listen, negotiate or compromise before making the final decision.	The parent takes the child seriously to reach a common preference and respects the child's autonomy.
The parent operates from some standard of what is in the child's 'best interest' or 'own good'.	The parent operates from the principle that autonomous humans of all ages are the ultimate best judge of their own best interest and assumes that coercion damages the ability to think rationally.
Parents may offer loving guidance within a framework of boundaries.	Parents believe that love is not a good reason to compromise another's autonomy. Love does not justify abandoning morality.
Various frameworks are used to supply the boundaries. These may be so-called 'natural' consequences, 'common sense', inherited memes, religious	There are no artificial boundaries. The participants use rationality and creativity to reach common preferences and create new knowledge to solve problems.

or ideological frameworks or (most often), a combination of the above.	
Parents regularly have outcomes in mind, both in terms of short term desired behaviour or long term general attributes.	Parents do not attempt to either prescribe or predict outcomes.
Parents decide ahead of solutions being sought that some problems are intractable and not capable of 'win-win' outcomes, so they must sometimes impose a solution in which only some win or a compromise in which no-one wins.	Parents believe that there are always solutions. They hold that sometimes we fail to find solutions because of our limited creativity and rationality and because we are fallible, but they assume that solutions, (in which all win), are, at least theoretically, always possible.
Parents may posit a 'contract' between them-selves and their children in which they provide food, warmth, shelter, protection and acceptance whilst their children owe various levels of duty or obedience.	Parents acknowledge an asymmetrical relationship between themselves and their children, in which their parental responsibility is not matched by a corresponding duty or obligation on the part of children who were never free to decide to enter, (or not), into such a contract.
Coercion is sometimes used as being preferable to some other bad, which is perceived as worse, (e.g. forced tooth brushing is better than possible tooth decay).	Parents do not believe that it is right to act immorally in order to obtain a good outcome.
Parents often believe that they are better placed to make decisions for their children on the basis of superior experience.	Parents non-coercively offer their experience, but do not assume that they are right. Whilst experience can be useful, it can also be fallible and subject to previous coercion damage, so all participants should subject all input to a process of conjecture and refutation. Lack of experience should not be used to dehumanise children or to make

	them appear less that full autonomous moral agents.
Children who get what they want become spoiled and selfish. Parents are in position best to know the limits of their resources and to make it clear that children cannot 'have everything'.	A spoilt child is a child in distress who can never be satisfied. Parents assume that children can be both 'self-centred' and act morally and that these things are not mutually exclusive. Parents realise that getting what we want is not equivalent to having everything. The aim is not immediately to meet every demand, but to find creative common preference solutions.
Parents may impose boundaries out of a fear of self-sacrifice or being coerced by their children.	Parents recognise that the balance of power rests with them and that they need to redress this imbalance. The aim is always to achieve mutual consent and find common preference solutions. Self-sacrifice may sometimes be a failure default, but is not to be tolerated as a chronic or regular outcome.
Parents assume that there are certain things that children just have to be taught. It is irresponsible of parents not to ensure that these 'basics' are learned, even if this sometimes means resorting to coercion.	Parents recognise that if there were such a list of 'essential things children must learn' then coercive parenting theories would be able to agree on what this list must contain, but there is no such agreement. Parents assume that if certain things are important or essential for children to survive in modern society, then there is no reason why a rational, creative, autonomous child would not learn them without coercion.
Parents assume that childhood is a preparation for life in the real or adult world and it is the parents' responsibility to equip children for this.	Parents assume that children's present life is intrinsically valuable of itself and that finding solutions to today's problems is not only the best way to live now, but will also tend to assist children to remain creative, flexible problem-solvers.

Taking Children Seriously is the only philosophy that does not damage autonomy and which allows for a consistently positive framework for negotiating family living and learning. It is a moral and educational paradigm, which furnishes families not with a list of guidelines, but with a process for solving problems in which everyone wins and learning never ends.

References and further reading

Clarke, Arthur C. (July 1973) *2001, A Space Odyssey*, London: Arrow Books

Dobson, James (1993) *Dare to Discipline*, Vida Publishing

Fortune-Wood, Jan (2000) *Doing it Their Way*, Nottingham: Educational Heretics Press

Haak, Carl *from* www.rsglh.org.parental.discipline.html

Lawrence, Sarah *articles in TCS Journal & website www.tcs.ac*

Liedlof, Jean (1989) *The Continuum Concept*, Arkana

Popper, Karl (1995) *The Myth of the Framework*, London: Routledge

Popper, Karl (1995) *In Search of a Better World*, London: Routledge

Websites to which reference is made:

www.attachmentparenting.org
www.gn.apc.org/edheretics
www.home-education.org.uk
www.parenting.org
www.positiveparenting.com
www.tcs.ac

Films to which reference is made:

Liar, Liar (1997) Universal City Studios

The Matrix (1999) Warner Brothers, Village Roadshow Films (BV) Ltd.